FIX-IT and FORGET-IT®

NEW COOKBOOK

Country French Vegetables, page 248

FIX-IT and FORGET-IT®

NEW COOKBOOK

250 new delicous
slow cooker recipes!

New York Times bestselling author
Phyllis Good

Good Books

Intercourse, PA 17534
800/762-7171
www.GoodBooks.com

Acknowledgments

This book has not been a one-person undertaking by any means. Margaret and Cliff have helped to make these recipes workable and readable. Tony and PJ tended to innumerable details. Taylor and other staff from The Good Cooking Store prepped and prepped. And prepped. Bonne and her helpers—and Jeremy—found the light in each recipe. Merle, Kate, and Rebecca believed in and encouraged this project along from its very first breath.

I can't imagine working without a team. How am I so fortunate? I am grateful to each of you.
                                                                    —*Phyllis*

Photography by Jeremy Hess
Design by Cliff Snyder

FIX-IT AND FORGET-IT® NEW COOKBOOK
Copyright © 2013 by Good Books, Intercourse, PA 17534

International Standard Book Number: 978-1-56148-800-1
Library of Congress Catalog Control Number: 2013943873

Publisher's Cataloging-in-Publication Data
Good, Phyllis Pellman
    Fix it and forget it new cookbook : 250 new delicious slow cooker recipes / Phyllis Pellman Good.
        p. cm.
        ISBN 978-1-56148-800-1
1. Electric cooking, slow. 2. Cookbooks. I. Fix it and forget it new cookbook : two hundred fifty new delicious slow cooker recipes. II. Title.

TX827 .G64 2013
641.5/884 --dc23   2013943873

Table of Contents

A couple of things upfront—

- **Remember, your slow cooker works for you.**

  It's capable of a lot more than you might have imagined.

  So don't be shy about what you ask it to do—like make cakes and breads and breakfast while you sleep.

  Or help you cook a meal for guests while you're all away enjoying a movie or football game together.

  Or relieve your pressure when you're hosting the whole family for a holiday meal.

  These are near-miracle appliances, especially if you understand a little bit about how they work. Here a few things I learned along the way.

- **Let's get rid of two myths right now—**

  Myth #1 "Slow cookers are a winter-time appliance." That's just ¼ of the truth.

  Remember that they can do their quiet slow work without

Deep, Dark, and Delicious Barbecue Sandwiches, page 116.

heating up your kitchen in the summertime. And they're just as happy cooking for you while you're at the pool with your kids or working in your lawn or garden.

Slow cookers will definitely work for you year-round.

These are near-miracle appliances.

Myth #2 "The main thing to make in them is beef stew." That's only $\frac{1}{10}$ of the truth, maybe less.

Flip through this book and you'll find recipes for all parts of a meal—all quick and easy to make, with ingredients you already have in your cupboards or which you can easily find in your nearby grocery store.

Which slow cooker is best for my household?

• **Size?** If you're part of a 4-person household (2 adults and 2 kids under 12), you'll probably be happy with a 4-quart size. You'll be able to fit in a couple of chicken legs and thighs or a small to medium beef roast.

Green Beans in Spicy Sauce, page 234.

Me? I like a 5-quart cooker, although I cook mostly for two adults these days. But I like leftovers—and I like to be able to make enough food to feed our kids when they come home.

There are advantages, too, to a 6- or 7-quart cooker. I think of three—

1. You can cook a turkey breast, turkey thighs, a whole chicken, or a good-sized beef roast in one of these.

2. You can fit a loaf pan or a baking dish into a 6- or 7-quart, depending on the shape of your cooker. That allows you to make bread or cakes, or even smaller quantities of main dishes, in your big-boy cooker. (Take your favorite baking dish and loaf pan along when you shop for a cooker to make sure they'll fit inside.)

3. You can feed a big group or produce freezer meals in addition to tonight's dinner.

Disadvantages of a 6- or 7-quart cooker? They take up more storage room. They don't fit as neatly into a dishwasher. If you usually cook only 2-4 quarts of food, these babies will tend to overcook quantities of less than 5 quarts. Better borrow your neighbor's for those rare occasions when you're cooking more.

What about a 1- to 3-quart size? They're great for lots of appetizers, for serving hot drinks, for baking cakes straight in the crock, and for sending with your college kid to the dorm. But be warned—food in smaller quantities tends to cook more quickly than larger amounts. So keep watch.

Think about having several slow cookers, each a different size. Then you can make a bunch of dishes at once for a whole meal, and you can pick the size that fits your immediate need. Maybe you're hosting a backyard barbecue or you're off to a potluck. Or you want to serve a few appetizers during a football game, or you've invited your child's soccer team home for hot sandwiches after a tournament.

• **Shape?** Ovals accommodate most shapes and cuts of meat. They also have more floor space, so if you're "baking" stuffed apples or saucing pork chops and don't want to stack them, an oval shape helps with that.

Think about having several slow cookers, each a different size.

• **Programmable, probe, or manual?** I really don't like dry, overcooked meat. That's why I'm a great believer in using quick-read meat thermometers. And that's why I'm drawn to slow cookers with a probe which allows you to select the internal temperature that you want. When it's reached, the slow cooker will automatically shift to Warm.

Programmable cookers allow you a good bit of control, too. You set the exact cooking time that you want and choose High or Low. The cooker switches to Warm when the cooking time is up.

- **Other handy features?** If you're planning to carry a cooker full of food in the car, you'll be happier if you have a lid that locks.

A big point—

Easy Spinach Quiche, page 293.

Learn to know your slow cooker. Plan a little get-acquainted time. Each slow cooker has its own personality—just like your oven (and your car).

Plus, many new slow cookers cook hotter and faster than earlier models. I think that with all of the concern for food safety, the slow cooker manufacturers have amped up their settings so that "High," "Low," and "Warm" are all higher temperatures than in the older models. That means they cook hotter—and therefore, faster—than the first slow cookers. The beauty of these little machines is that they're supposed to cook low and slow. We count on that when we flip the switch in the morning before we leave the house for 10 hours or so.

So—because none of us knows what kind of temperament our slow cooker has until we try it out, nor how hot it cooks—don't assume anything.

Save yourself a disappointment and make the first recipe in your new slow cooker on a day when you're at home. Cook it for the shortest amount of time the recipe calls for. Then check the food to see if it's done. Or if you start smelling food that seems to be finished, turn off the cooker and rescue your food.

Then write in your cookbook, next to the recipe you made, exactly how long it took to cook it. The next time you make it, you won't need to try to remember.

And apply what you learned to the next recipes you make in your cooker. If another recipe says it needs to cook 7-9 hours, and you've discovered you own a fast and furious model, cook that recipe for 6-6½ hours and then check it. You can always cook a recipe longer; too bad you can't reverse things if you've overdone it.

- **Slow-cooked food doesn't have to taste over-cooked.** You don't have to sacrifice the cooker's convenience to take care of that. But there are a few tricks that allow you to have more control over the outcome.

What to do about a too-hot, too-fast slow cooker?

So what can you do when you're gone for 9 hours, but want to make a recipe that cooks for only 6 hours?

1. If you've got a slow cooker that flips automatically to Warm after it's cooked your dinner, let it do that. But know that the food may be somewhat overcooked since Warm settings for most cookers are 165°F.

2. My friend, who can't bear overcooked food, often cooks Tuesday night's meal on Monday evening. When she walks in the door after work on Monday, she flips on the cooker. She figures she has 6 to 7 hours until she goes to bed. If the food's finished in a shorter amount of time, she's there to flip it off before it overcooks.

She puts the cooked food in the fridge. Tuesday evening she heats the already-cooked food in the microwave.

And so on throughout the week.

3. Take your slow cooker to work with you, if your situation allows for this. Then you can turn it on and off when you need to. Some slow cookers have locking lids so you don't need to worry as much about spills. You can get snuggly insulated carrier totes which keep them warm on the drive home.

Of course, be prepared for longing looks from your co-workers as the afternoon wears on.

4. When your kids are old enough to take the food from the fridge, to put it into the cooker, and to flip it on when they get home from school, ask them to do it.

Or if an adult works at home, tell him or her when to turn on the cooker.

Two kinds of recipes in this book

• **Quick and Easy**

Some days I have no space in my head to think, let alone make a grocery list or cook. I need a recipe that makes itself. We've marked those kinds of recipes throughout the book, "Quick and Easy." And we made a "Quick and Easy Recipe Index" on page 374. Flip there for the list, drop your finger on any of those recipes, and you've got dinner. Well, almost.

Salmon-Stuffed Mushrooms, page 305.

• **A Little More Challenging**

Sometimes I'm looking for a little more challenge in the kitchen. I'm ready to do a bit of browning, some more involved prep, even adding ingredients to the slow cooker in stages. We've got those recipes here, too.

So find the recipes that match your mood— or the time you have available to prep.

I'm cheering you on! You absolutely can make great food at home with these recipes!

Phyllis Good

Your Slow Cooker Guidebook –
Things you'll be happier knowing!

1. Slow cookers tend to work best when they're ⅔ full. You may need to increase the cooking time if you've exceeded that amount, or reduce it if you've put in less than that.

   If you're going to exceed that limit, pull out your second slow cooker (what – you have only one?!) and divide the contents between them.

Fudgy Chocolate Cake, page 316.

2. Cut the hard veggies going into your cooker into chunks of about equal size. In other words, make your potato and carrot pieces about the same size. Then they'll be done cooking at nearly the same time. Softer veggies, like bell peppers and zucchini, cook faster, so they don't need to be cut as small. But again, keep them similar in size, too, to each other so they finish together.

3. Because raw vegetables are notoriously tough customers in a slow cooker, layer them over the bottom and around the sides of the cooker, as much as possible. That puts them in more direct contact with the heat.

4. Important things to remember that don't show up in recipes:
   • The fuller your slow cooker, the longer it will take its contents to cook.
   • The more densely packed the cooker's contents are, the longer they will take to cook.
   • The larger the chunks of meat or vegetables, the more time they will need to cook.

5. Use only the amount of liquid called for in a recipe. In contrast to an oven or a stovetop, a slow cooker tends to draw juices out of food and then harbor it.

    Of course, if you sense that the food in your cooker is drying out, or browning excessively before it finishes cooking, you may want to add ½ cup of warm liquid to the cooker.

6. There are consequences to lifting the lid on your slow cooker while it's cooking. To compensate for the lost heat, you should plan to add 15-20 minutes of cooking time for each time the lid was lifted off.

    On the other hand, moisture gathers in a slow cooker as it works. To allow that to cook off, or to thicken the cooking juices, take the lid off during the last half hour of cooking time.

7. If you have a big slow cooker (7- to 8-qt.), you can cook a small batch in it by putting the recipe ingredients into an oven-safe baking dish or baking pan and then placing that into the cooker's *crock*. First, put a trivet or some metal jar rings on the bottom of the *crock*, and then set your dish or pan on top of them. Or a loaf pan may "hook onto" the top ridges of the *crock* belonging to a large oval cooker and hang there straight and securely, "baking" a cake or quick bread. Cover the cooker and flip it on.

8. A working slow cooker gets hot on the outside – and I mean the outer electrical unit as well as the inner vessel. Make sure that curious and unsuspecting children or adults don't grab hold of either part. Use oven mitts when lifting any part of a hot cooker.

9. You must absolutely use a quick-read meat thermometer! That will end over-cooking (or under-cooking) your beef and pork roasts, turkey breasts, and chicken thighs. How do you know, otherwise?

    Don't put frozen food in your slow cooker.

    Internal Cooking Temperatures:
    Beef—125-130°F (rare); 140-145°F (medium); 160°F (well-done)
    Pork—140-145°F (rare); 145-150°F (medium); 160°F (well-done)
    Turkey and Chicken—165°F

10. Add fresh herbs 10 minutes before the end of the cooking time to maximize their flavor.

11. If your recipe calls for cooked pasta, add it 10 minutes before the end of the cooking time if the cooker is on High; 30 minutes before the end of the cooking time if it's on Low. Then the pasta won't get mushy.

12. If your recipe calls for sour cream or cream, stir it in 5 minutes before the end of the cooking time. You want it to heat but not boil or simmer.

13. Don't put frozen food into your slow cooker. It should always be thawed. Otherwise, you risk food poisoning since the food will take longer to reach a safe cooking temperature.

14. Approximate Slow Cooker Temperatures:
    - High—212°F–300°F (Remember, each slow cooker is different.)
    - Low—170°F–200°F
    - Simmer—185°F
    - Warm—165°F

15. One hour of cooking on High is about equal to 2½ hours of cooking on Low.

16. Cooked and dried bean measurements:
    - 16-oz. can, drained = about 1¾ cups beans
    - 19-oz. can, drained = about 2 cups beans
    - 1 lb. dried beans (about 2½ cups) = 5 cups cooked beans
    Cooked beans freeze well. Store them in freezer bags (squeeze the air out first) or freezer boxes.

Slow Cooker Basic Beans, page 354.

Main Dishes

Chicken and Turkey

Herbed Chicken, page 27

Parmigiana Chicken

Makes 6 servings
Prep. Time: 20-30 minutes ❧ *Cooking Time: 2-6 hours*
Ideal slow-cooker size: 4-quart

1 egg

1 tsp. salt

¼ tsp. pepper

6 bone-in, skinless chicken breast halves

1 cup Italian bread crumbs

2–4 Tbsp. butter

14-oz. jar of your favorite pizza sauce

6 slices mozzarella cheese

grated Parmesan cheese

1. In a low-sided bowl, big enough to dip a chicken breast half into, beat egg, salt, and pepper together.

2. Put bread crumbs in another low-sided bowl, also big enough to hold a chicken breast half.

3. Dip each breast half into egg mixture. Drain.

4. Dip each breast half into bread crumbs and cover both sides.

5. Meanwhile, melt butter in skillet. Lightly brown each breast on both sides in butter in skillet. You can put several into the skillet at once, but make sure not to crowd the skillet or they won't brown.

6. Arrange browned chicken in slow cooker.

7. Spoon pizza sauce over chicken.

8. Cover cooker. Cook on Low 4–6 hours, or until chicken registers 165° on a meat thermometer stuck into the center of the breast, but not touching any bone.

9. Layer mozzarella cheese over top and sprinkle with Parmesan cheese. Cook uncovered, just until the cheese melts.

TIP

You can shred the chicken by using 2 forks to pull it apart, then mixing it and the cheesy, tomato-y sauce together.

Why I like this recipe —
It might sound a little bit fancy, but it's very simple and quick. Just don't overcook the breasts. It's easy to do. Put that handy-dandy easy-read thermometer to use. You'll be safe, and you'll have succulent meat.

Basil Chicken

Makes 4-6 servings
Prep. Time: 15 minutes   Cooking Time: 4½ hours
Ideal slow-cooker size: 4-quart

2 pounds boneless, skinless chicken thighs

14½-oz. can diced tomatoes with juice

14½-oz can garbanzo beans, drained and rinsed

2 Tbsp. capers with their brine

2 garlic cloves, sliced thinly

⅛ tsp. freshly ground black pepper

1 tsp. dried basil

8 oz. crumbled feta cheese

¼ cup tightly packed basil leaves, chopped

1. Place chicken in slow cooker. Pour tomatoes, garbanzos, and capers on top.
2. Sprinkle with garlic slices, pepper, and dried basil.
3. Cover and cook on Low 4 hours.
4. Sprinkle with feta. Cook on Low for 15–30 more minutes, or until chicken is done.
5. Sprinkle with fresh basil and serve. Great served with pasta or crusty bread to handle the sauce.

French Chicken

QUICK *and* EASY

Makes 4-6 servings
Prep. Time: 15 minutes ❦ *Cooking Time: 4½–5½ hours*
Ideal slow-cooker size: 5-quart

1 lb. baby carrots

2 medium onions, sliced

2 ribs celery, diced

4 garlic cloves, peeled

3 lbs. bone-in chicken thighs, skin removed

★ ½ cup white cooking wine *or* chicken stock

1½ tsp. salt

½ tsp. black pepper

1 tsp. dried basil

½ tsp. dried marjoram

2 Tbsp. chopped fresh parsley

★ TO MAKE YOUR OWN STOCK, SEE PAGE 357.

1. Place carrots, onions, celery, and garlic in bottom of slow cooker.
2. Lay chicken thighs on top. Pour wine or broth over chicken.
3. Sprinkle with salt, pepper, basil, and marjoram.
4. Cover. Cook on Low 4½–5½ hours, until chicken registers 165° on a meat thermometer and carrots are tender.
5. Sprinkle with fresh parsley before serving.

Why I like this recipe —
It is tempting to have
a little French daydream
when you make this chicken.
It's very simple, but the
flavor is wonderful—isn't
that how the French cook?

Simple Chicken Thighs

Makes 4-6 servings

Prep. Time: 10 minutes ❧ Cooking Time: 4-6 hours ❧ Chilling Time: 3-12 hours
Ideal slow-cooker size: 4-quart

2 lbs. bone-in chicken thighs, skin removed

2 Tbsp. olive oil

3 Tbsp. red wine vinegar

¼ cup honey

¼ cup soy sauce

1 garlic clove, minced

½ tsp. freshly ground pepper

¼ cup chopped fresh parsley

1. Place chicken in a shallow glass pan in a single layer.

2. In a small bowl, combine oil, vinegar, honey, soy sauce, garlic, pepper, and parsley.

3. Pour over chicken. Marinate in the fridge for at least 3 hours and up to 12.

4. Place chicken with marinade in slow cooker. Cover and cook on Low for 4-6 hours.

5. Either lift the chicken thighs out of the resulting sauce and serve, or thicken the sauce with a mixture of 1 Tbsp. cornstarch and 3 Tbsp. water whisked together, and then whisked through the hot sauce. Serve thickened sauce as a gravy on the side.

Why I like this recipe—
Soy sauce does wonderful things to meat. It's a tenderizer with good flavor. And this recipe is so versatile: serve the chicken as a main dish with gravy, baked potatoes and steamed broccoli, or slice it atop a green salad, or shred it as a filling for tortillas with lots of fun garnishes.

Favorite Honey Chicken

QUICK
and
EASY

Makes 6 servings
Prep. Time: 15 minutes ✂ Cooking Time: 4 hours
Ideal slow-cooker size: 4- or 5-quart

6 boneless, skinless chicken thighs

half a small onion, sliced in rings

4 Tbsp. butter

½ cup honey

¼ cup prepared mustard

½ tsp. salt

1 tsp. curry powder

1. Wash and pat chicken dry. Lay it in the slow cooker. Separate the onions into individual rings and distribute them among the chicken pieces.

2. Melt butter in the microwave. Mix well with remaining ingredients and pour over chicken.

3. Cover and cook on Low for 4 hours, or until chicken registers 165° on a meat thermometer. If you have time and inclination, place the chicken and sauce on a rimmed baking sheet and run under the broiler to get some browned spots on the chicken and bubbly sauce.

Chicken Cacciatore

Makes 6 servings
Prep. Time: 15 minutes ❧ Cooking Time: 5-6 hours
Ideal slow-cooker size: 5-quart

3 lbs. bone-in chicken pieces, skin removed

2 green bell peppers, thinly sliced

2 medium onions, thinly sliced

2 garlic cloves, thinly sliced

½ lb. fresh mushrooms, sliced

½ tsp. dried rosemary

1 tsp. dried oregano

½ tsp. dried basil

1 tsp. salt

¼ tsp. pepper, freshly ground

1 Tbsp. balsamic vinegar

1 cup tomato sauce

3 cups chopped tomatoes

3 oz. tomato paste

2-oz. can sliced black olives, drained

¾ cup chopped fresh basil, *optional*

hot cooked spaghetti

1. Lay chicken pieces in slow cooker. Add peppers, onions, garlic, and mushrooms.
2. In a bowl, mix together rosemary, oregano, dried basil, salt, pepper, vinegar, tomato sauce, tomatoes, and tomato paste.
3. Pour tomato mixture over vegetables and chicken.
4. Cover and cook on Low for 5-6 hours, until chicken is tender and done.
5. Serve chicken pieces and sauce over spaghetti in soup plates, sprinkled with olives and optional basil.

Why I like this recipe —
   This is comfort food for my family. The gentle, moist heat of the slow cooker makes the chicken and sauce so succulent. I almost always add a few slices of bread to the table so we can wipe up every bit of the delicious sauce.

Asian Chicken Breast

Makes 4 servings
Prep. Time: 10–15 minutes ❦ Cooking Time: 4 hours
Ideal slow-cooker size: 3½- or 4-quart

1 Tbsp. sesame oil

1 Tbsp. rice vinegar *or*
white wine vinegar

3 Tbsp. soy sauce

3 Tbsp. honey

fresh ground pepper, to taste

2" piece ginger root,
chopped, peeled *or* not

1 lb. boneless skinless
chicken breasts

2 spring onions, chopped

3 Tbsp. sesame seeds, toasted

1. Mix together sesame oil, vinegar, soy sauce, honey, and pepper until smooth.

2. Place chicken and ginger in slow cooker. Pour sauce on top, spreading it to distribute evenly.

3. Cover and cook on Low for 4 hours, until chicken is just cooked.

4. Remove chicken and sauce to serving platter. Sprinkle with spring onions and sesame seeds. Lovely served with hot rice.

TIP

To toast the sesame seeds, spread them in a small tray or pan. Place in 350° oven or toaster oven for 5–7 minutes until lightly tan and scented.

Why I like this recipe—
It's just so tasty and easy. The garnishes really make the finished chicken look special; in fact, I frequently garnish slow cooker dishes with something green because we eat with our eyes, too!

Herbed Chicken

Makes 4–6 servings
Prep. Time: 15 minutes ❦ Cooking Time: 4–6 hours
Ideal slow-cooker size: 6-quart

5-lb. roasting chicken

1 onion, quartered

2 garlic cloves:
1 sliced, 1 whole

1 Tbsp. fresh parsley,
or 1 tsp. dried

1 Tbsp. fresh sage,
or 1 tsp. dried

1 Tbsp. fresh rosemary,
or 1 tsp. dried

1 Tbsp. fresh thyme,
or 1 tsp. dried

1 Tbsp. butter, softened

paprika to taste

salt to taste

pepper to taste

1. Clean and wash the chicken. Pat dry.
2. Put the quartered onion and sliced garlic into the bird's cavity. Stuff in the parsley, sage, rosemary, and thyme, too.
3. Rub the outside of the chicken with the whole garlic clove, and then toss it into the cavity.
4. Rub the outside of the chicken with softened butter. Sprinkle with paprika, salt and pepper.
5. Place chicken into the greased slow cooker.
6. Cover. Cook on Low 4–6 hours, or until the meat is tender, the drumsticks move freely, and the juices run clear.
7. Lift the chicken out of the cooker onto a platter. Cover with foil to keep warm. Let it stand for 15 minutes before cutting it up.
8. Thicken the chicken stock to make gravy. Or use the broth to make rice.

Why I like this recipe —
    You can't get to Provence this year?! Try this instead.
Stop thinking that pesto is fancy food. You can make it
anytime of the year, even if you don't have fresh basil.

Herby Chicken with Pesto

Makes 6-8 servings
Prep. Time: 20 minutes ❧ Cooking Time: 4–6 hours
Ideal slow-cooker size: 6-quart

PESTO INGREDIENTS:

2 cups fresh basil, *or* 2 Tbsp. dried basil

½ cup olive oil

2 Tbsp. pine nuts

2 cloves garlic, crushed

1 tsp. salt

½ cup Parmesan cheese, freshly grated

2 Tbsp. Romano cheese, grated

3 Tbsp. butter, softened

CHICKEN INGREDIENTS:

6 medium onions, coarsely chopped

2 Tbsp. olive oil

2 28-oz. cans plum tomatoes, undrained

1 Tbsp. fresh thyme, *or* 1 tsp. dried thyme

1 Tbsp. fresh basil, *or* 1 tsp. dried basil

1 Tbsp. fresh tarragon, *or* 1 tsp. dried tarragon

1 Tbsp. fresh rosemary, *or* 1 tsp. fresh rosemary

4 cloves fresh garlic, minced

★ 2 cups chicken broth

4 cups dry white wine

2–3 lbs. chicken thighs, bone in, skin removed

1½–2 lbs. small new potatoes, unpeeled

2 loaves French bread, sliced and warmed

★ TO MAKE YOUR OWN BROTH, SEE PAGE 357.

1. Make the pesto first. Blend all of its ingredients together, except the cheeses and softened butter, in a blender or food processor. Pour the mixture into a bowl and then stir in the cheeses and butter.

2. Put the onions, olive oil, tomatoes with their juice, all the herbs, the garlic, chicken broth, wine, and half the pesto into your slow cooker. Mix everything together well.

3. Nestle the chicken thighs into the tomato-y broth, submerging them as much as you can.

4. Add the potatoes, pushing them down into the broth, too.

5. Cover. Cook on Low 4–6 hours, or until the potatoes are soft when you jag them with a fork and the chicken is tender.

6. Serve in deep soup plates with plenty of hot French bread to mop up the juices. Serve the remaining pesto at the table.

Creamy Chicken in Gravy

Makes 6 servings
Prep. Time: 10 minutes ❦ Cooking Time: 3-6 hours
Ideal slow-cooker size: 4-quart

6 large bone-in chicken thighs, skin removed

★ 10¾-oz. can cream of broccoli, *or* broccoli cheese, soup

★ 10¾-oz. can cream of chicken soup

½ cup white wine

½ tsp. dried thyme

¼ tsp. dried sage

pinch dried rosemary

pinch black pepper

¼ lb. fresh mushrooms, sliced, *or* 4-oz. can sliced mushrooms, undrained

---

★ TO MAKE YOUR OWN CREAM SOUPS, SEE PAGES 370-371

1. Place chicken thighs in slow cooker.
2. In bowl mix together soups, wine, herbs, and mushroom slices. Pour over chicken.
3. Cover. Cook on Low 4-5 hours, or until chicken is tender but not dry.
4. Serve over rice or noodles.

*Why I like this recipe —
This is plain down good
and comforting. If you go
the quick soup route, you
can make this almost
without thinking.*

Chicken with Raisins and Rice

Makes 8 servings
Prep. Time: 15-20 minutes ❧ *Cooking Time: 2½-5½ hours*
Ideal slow-cooker size: 5-quart

3 cups unsalted, low-fat chicken broth

1½ cups uncooked, long-grain white rice

¾ cup raisins

½ cup chopped onion

2-3 lbs. chicken thighs, bone in, skin removed

½ cup all-purpose flour

1 Tbsp. curry powder

½ tsp. salt

½ cup chopped peanuts

1. Combine chicken broth, rice, raisins, and onions in your greased slow cooker.
2. Combine flour, curry, and salt in a sturdy plastic bag without any holes or tears. Add chicken thighs, one at a time, to the bag and shake until well coated. Lay each piece in the rice mixture, pushing it down until it's as submerged as possible.
3. Cover. Cook on Low 4-5 hours, or on High 2-3 hours.
4. Lift the chicken onto a platter. Cover with foil to keep warm. Stir the peanuts into the rice. Put the chicken back into the cooker. Cover and cook ½ hour longer.

Why I like this recipe —
This is a one-pot dish. And you don't need to cook the rice ahead of time. Jack up the curry, onions, raisins, or peanuts if you want to increase the flavor. Once again, you can customize the recipe to suit whoever you're feeding.

Chicken Breasts Stuffed with Pesto

Makes 6 servings
Prep. Time: 30 minutes   ✿   Cooking Time: 4–6 hours
Ideal slow-cooker size: 6-quart

6 boneless, skinless
chicken breasts,
not more than
4 lbs. total

½ cup chopped
fresh basil

6 garlic cloves

⅓ cup extra-virgin
olive oil

½ cup grated
Parmesan cheese

¾ cup fresh
bread crumbs

hot water, *optional*

2 Tbsp. pine nuts

watercress, *optional*

1. Flatten each chicken breast by pounding between two sheets of wax paper, until they're each ½" thick. Lay each one on a square, buttered piece of tin foil, shiny side up.

2. In a food processor, mix together basil, garlic, and olive oil. Pulse several times to chop and blend the ingredients.

3. Add cheese and bread crumbs. Process until the mixture forms a paste. Add a little bit of hot water if you need it to make the paste spreadable. Add the pine nuts and pulse to chop.

4. Divide the basil mixture among the 8 breasts. Place a spoonful on the center of each breast. Roll up each stuffed breast jelly-roll style. Wrap the square of foil tightly around each one to hold the goodies inside.

5. Stack the foil packages of chicken evenly in the cooker. Cook 4–6 hours on Low. After 4 hours, lift a pack out of the cooker and open carefully. Open the package so that the steam is directed away from yourself. Stick the quick-read meat thermometer into the center of the breast (be sure you're against meat and not the filling). If the thermometer registers 165°, the chicken is finished. If it's less than that, wrap it up, put it back in the cooker, and continue cooking for another 30 minutes. Repeat the check.

6. When the chicken is done cooking, remove each breast from the foil. Slice it into 1"-thick slices, fanning them over a dinner plate. Spoon some cooking juices over top.

7. If you want, strew some fresh watercress leaves over top before serving.

Curried Chicken and Fruit

Makes 5 servings

Prep. Time: 20 minutes ❧ Cooking Time: 4¼ to 5¼ hours

Ideal slow-cooker size: 5-quart

2½–3½ lbs. chicken thighs,
bone in, skin removed

½ tsp. salt

¼ tsp. pepper

1–2 Tbsp. curry powder,
depending on how
much you like curry

1 garlic clove,
crushed *or* minced

1 Tbsp. butter, melted

★ ½ cup chicken broth, *or*
1 chicken bouillon cube
dissolved in ½ cup water

2 Tbsp. finely chopped onion

29-oz. can sliced peaches

½ cup pitted prunes

3 Tbsp. cornstarch

3 Tbsp. cold water

cooked rice, for serving

peanuts, shredded
coconut, and fresh
pineapple chunks,
optional, for serving

★ TO MAKE YOUR OWN STOCK, SEE PAGE 357.

1. Place chicken in slow cooker.

2. Combine salt, pepper, curry powder, garlic, butter, broth, and onions in bowl.

3. Drain peaches, reserving syrup. Add ½ cup syrup to curry mixture. Pour over chicken.

4. Cover. Cook on Low 4–5 hours. Remove chicken from slow cooker. Tent with foil to keep warm.

5. Turn cooker on High. Stir prunes into sauce in cooker.

6. In a small bowl, dissolve cornstarch in cold water. Stir into hot broth in slow cooker.

7. Cover. Cook on High 10 minutes, stirring once or twice, or until thickened. Add peaches. Add cooked chicken. (You can debone the chicken if you want.)

8. Serve over cooked rice. Offer peanuts, shredded coconut, and fresh pineapple chunks as condiments.

Wild Rice with Chicken

QUICK
and
EASY

Makes 8-10 servings
Prep. Time: 20 minutes ✂ *Cooking Time: 4-8 hours*
Ideal slow-cooker size: 4-quart

2 cups wild rice, uncooked

½ cup chopped onions

½ cup chopped celery

2 cups uncooked skinless chicken thighs, cut in 1-inch pieces

★ 6 cups chicken stock

¼-½ tsp. salt, depending how salty your stock is

¼ tsp. pepper

¼ tsp. garlic powder

½ tsp. dried sage

8-12-oz. canned mushrooms, drained, or ½ lb. fresh mushrooms, sliced

½ cup slivered almonds

2 Tbsp. fresh parsley

★ TO MAKE YOUR OWN STOCK, SEE PAGE 357.

1. Wash and drain rice.
2. Combine all ingredients, except mushrooms, almonds, and parsley, in greased slow cooker. Mix well.
3. Cover. Cook on Low 4-8 hours, or until rice is tender. Don't lift the lid to check on things until the rice has cooked 4 hours.
4. Ten minutes before the end of the cooking time, stir in the mushrooms. Cover and continue cooking.
5. Just before serving, stir in slivered almonds. Garnish with fresh parsley.

Sunny Chicken

Makes 4-5 servings

Prep. Time: 20-30 minutes ❦ *Cooking Time: 4-6 hours*

Ideal slow-cooker size: 6-quart

1 large onion, sliced into thin rings, *divided*

3 sweet, juicy oranges, each cut into thin slices, *divided*

3 lemons, thinly sliced, *divided*

3 limes, thinly sliced, *divided*

9 fresh rosemary sprigs, *divided*

2 Tbsp. minced garlic, *divided*

5-lb. chicken

salt and pepper to taste

1. Layer ⅓ of the onion slices, 1 sliced orange, 1 sliced lemon, and 1 sliced lime into your slow cooker. Top with 3 rosemary sprigs and ⅓ of the minced garlic.

2. Stuff with half the remaining onion slices, 1 sliced orange, 1 sliced lemon, and 1 sliced lime, half the remaining garlic and 3 rosemary sprigs. Place the stuffed chicken—upside down—in your slow cooker. (That helps to keep the breast meat from drying out.)

3. Sprinkle with plenty of salt and pepper. Spread the rest of the onion, orange, lemon, and lime slices, and the remaining garlic and rosemary sprigs around the chicken and on top of it.

4. Cover. Cook on Low 4-6 hours, or until meat is tender but not dry.

5. Remove chicken from cooker and place rightside up on rimmed baking sheet. Place under broiler until top is nicely browned, only a minute or so, watching closely.

6. Cover chicken with foil for 15 minutes. Then carve, put the pieces on a platter, and spoon the citrus and onion slices over top before serving.

Savory Cranberry Chicken

Makes 6 servings
Prep. Time: 20 minutes   Cooking Time: 4 hours
Ideal slow-cooker size: 5-quart

1 cup chopped onion

2 tsp. vegetable oil

6 boneless, skinless chicken breast halves

⅓ cup tomato sauce

1 Tbsp. cider vinegar

1 Tbsp. brown sugar

2 Tbsp. orange marmalade

½ cup dried cranberries

½ tsp. chili powder

½ tsp. ground allspice

1 tsp. salt

¼ tsp. freshly ground pepper

1. Place onion, oil, and a few chicken breast halves in a large skillet. Brown the halves about 3 minutes on each side. Be careful not to crowd the skillet with the chicken or it will steam, not brown.

2. Remove the onions if they are browned and place in slow cooker. Continue to brown the chicken in batches (along with the onions if you wish) until all the halves are browned on both sides.

3. Mix remaining ingredients in a small bowl until smooth.

4. Pour sauce over chicken breasts.

5. Cover and cook on Low for about 4 hours, until chicken registers 165° on a meat thermometer stuck into the centers of the breasts.

6. Serve over brown rice to catch and enjoy the lovely sauce.

Why I like this recipe—
I have fond memories of assembling this dish before going on a chilly hike (just brisk enough to keep warm!) with dear friends, and returning to this beautiful cranberry chicken for supper.

Amish Filling

Makes 8-10 servings

Prep. Time: 40-45 minutes ❦ *Cooking Time: 3-4 hours*

Ideal slow-cooker size: 6- or 7-quart

1½ sticks (12 Tbsp.) butter

1 medium onion, diced

2 cups diced celery

1½ tsp. salt

½ tsp. pepper

4 eggs, beaten

★ 3-4 cups chicken broth, *divided*

18-20 slices bread (about 12-14 cups), cubed *or* torn

4 cups diced, cooked chicken, *divided*

★ TO MAKE YOUR OWN BROTH, SEE PAGE 357.

1. Melt the butter in a large stockpot (you'll soon see why you need the big pot). Sauté the onion and celery, stirring often, until the vegetables are just softened. Stir in the salt and pepper.

2. In a medium-sized bowl, mix the eggs and 2 cups chicken broth together.

3. Put the bread pieces into a large bowl. Pour the eggs-and-broth mixture, and the butter with the sautéed onions and celery, over the bread cubes. Toss everything together until all of the bread is moistened.

4. Spoon the bread cubes into the large stockpot (that you used in Step 1) and fry over medium heat until lightly browned. Stir often so the bread cubes brown throughout and so none burn.

5. When the bread is nicely browned, spoon about ⅓ of it into your large, greased slow cooker.

6. Top it with half the chicken.

7. Put half the remaining bread into the slow cooker. Top with the rest of the chicken. Add the rest of the bread on top.

8. Pour 1 cup chicken broth across the top layer of bread. You can add more broth while the Filling cooks if you want it to stay really moist.

9. Cover. Cook on Low 3-4 hours. The longer the Filling cooks, the drier it will be. Or if you don't have time to let it cook longer but like it somewhat dry, take the lid off for the last 45 minutes of cooking.

TIP

Though it's not in the traditional Amish recipe, you can add dried sage and thyme to Step 1 if you like.

"Stir-Fry" Chicken and Broccoli

Makes 4 servings
Prep. Time: 20 minutes ❧ Cooking Time: 1-3 hours
Ideal slow-cooker size: 4-quart

4 good-sized boneless, skinless chicken thighs

1–2 Tbsp. oil

½ cup picante sauce

2 Tbsp. soy sauce

½ tsp. sugar

½ Tbsp. quick-cooking tapioca

1 medium onion, chopped

2 garlic cloves, minced

½ tsp. ground ginger

2 cups broccoli florets

1 medium red bell pepper, cut into pieces

1. Cut chicken into 1" cubes and brown lightly in oil in skillet. Place in slow cooker.
2. Stir in remaining ingredients.
3. Cover. Cook on High 1-1½ hours or on Low 2-3 hours.
4. Serve over cooked white rice.

TIP

Use this recipe as an example for adapting your other favorite stir-fry recipes.

Cornish Game Hens with Bacon and New Potatoes

QUICK
and
EASY

Makes 4 servings

Prep. Time: 20 minutes ✻ *Cooking Time: 4–6 hours*

Ideal slow-cooker size: 6-quart

2 Cornish game hens

½ tsp. salt

1 tsp. dried thyme

1 tsp. dried rosemary

2 garlic cloves, peeled

2 carrots, scrubbed and cut in chunks

1½ cups small new potatoes, scrubbed and dried

4 slices bacon

1. Rub hens inside and out with salt, thyme, and rosemary. Place a garlic clove in each cavity.

2. Spread carrots and potatoes in slow cooker. Lay the hens on top.

3. Lay the bacon slices in a cross on each hen, tucking the ends under.

4. Cover and cook on Low for 4–6 hours, or until legs move easily when pulled on or twisted.

5. Before serving, brown and crisp the bacon by setting hens on a baking sheet and broiling for a minute or two, OR don't bother with the broiling and simply discard the bacon.

Why I like this recipe —
These petite little hens are elegant, delicious, and very simple. Impress some special people and accept the compliments—they don't need to know how easy it was!

Mexican Supper-in-a-Crock

Makes 8 servings
Prep. Time: 20 minutes ❧ *Cooking Time: 3-4 hours*
Ideal slow-cooker size: 5-quart

1 cup uncooked brown rice

★ 1½ cups chicken stock, and possibly ¼ cup more

1 lb. boneless, skinless chicken breast, cubed

¼ cup chopped onion

15-oz. can black beans, rinsed and drained

1 cup corn, canned, frozen, *or* fresh

4 garlic cloves, sliced thinly

1 cup diced red bell pepper

1 cup diced green bell pepper

14½-oz. can diced tomatoes, undrained

2 tsp. ground cumin

1 Tbsp. chili powder

½ tsp. salt, *or* less, depending on how salty your stock is

¼ tsp. pepper

1½ cups shredded Monterey Jack *or* pepper Jack cheese

½ cup chopped cilantro, for garnish

★ TO MAKE YOUR OWN STOCK, SEE PAGE 357.

1. Pour rice and 1½ cups stock together into lightly greased crock.

2. Put chicken cubes in next, followed by onion, black beans, corn, garlic, red pepper, and green pepper.

3. In a separate bowl, stir together tomatoes, cumin, chili powder, salt, and pepper. Pour evenly over the contents of the crock.

4. Cover and cook on High for 3 hours.

5. Gently poke a knife down to the bottom to see if rice is done. If it is, add the cheese on top and cook an additional 15 minutes until cheese is nicely melted. If the rice is still a little crunchy and there is no liquid left, add ¼ cup hot water or hot stock and cook an additional 30 minutes on High. Then add cheese and allow to melt for 15 minutes.

6. Sprinkle with chopped cilantro just before serving.

Arroz con Pollo

Makes 6-8 servings
Prep. Time: 25 minutes ❧ Cooking Time: 2½–3½ hours
Ideal slow-cooker size: 4-quart

1 Tbsp. vegetable oil

4 strips bacon, chopped

2 cups uncooked, diced boneless, skinless chicken breast

1 onion, chopped

1 green bell pepper, chopped

2 cups long-grain white rice, uncooked

3⅓ cups chicken broth

3 cloves garlic, minced

½ cup chopped fresh cilantro

¼ tsp. pepper

1 tsp. dried oregano

1 tsp. chili powder

½ tsp. turmeric

½ cup tomato sauce

½ cup sliced green olives

1 cup frozen peas, thawed

1. Heat oil in skillet. Add bacon, chicken, onion, pepper, and rice. Fry for several minutes to allow bacon to crisp up and chicken to get browned spots. Stir well to coat rice. Allow to brown for a few more minutes without stirring.

2. Scrape sauté into slow cooker, being sure to get all drippings and browned bits.

3. Add chicken broth, garlic, cilantro, pepper, oregano, chili powder, turmeric, and tomato sauce. Stir.

4. Cover and cook on High for 1½–2½ hours, until rice is tender and liquid is absorbed.

5. Use a fork to gently stir in olives and peas, fluffing up rice as you go. Allow to rest, covered, for a few minutes before serving.

Why I like this recipe —
I noticed a big pot of rice and chicken in the school office when I stopped by my girls' elementary school years ago — boy, it smelled good. An enterprising mother was selling Arroz con Pollo to the teachers and staff at lunchtime to make a little cash. I acquired a recipe of sorts in broken English, and I'm happy to say it converts quite nicely to the slow cooker.

Tex-Mex Chicken Roll-ups

Makes 6 servings

Prep. Time: 30 minutes ❦ Cooking Time: 4½–5 hours

Ideal slow-cooker size: 5- or 6-quart oval

6 boneless, skinless chicken breast halves, about 1½ lbs.

6 oz. Monterey Jack cheese, cut into 2"-long, ½"-thick sticks

2 4-oz. cans chopped green chilies, drained

¾ cup flour

½ cup (1 stick) butter, melted

½ cup dry bread crumbs

¼ cup grated Parmesan cheese

1 Tbsp. chili powder

pinch cayenne, *optional*

½ tsp. salt

½ tsp. ground cumin

1. Cover each chicken breast with plastic wrap, and on a cutting board, flatten each with a mallet to ⅛" thickness.
2. Place a cheese stick in the middle of each and top with a mound of chilies. Roll up and tuck in ends. Secure with toothpick. Set aside each breast half on a platter.
3. Place flour in a shallow dish, and melted butter in another.
4. In yet another shallow dish, mix together bread crumbs, Parmesan cheese, chili powder, optional cayenne, salt, and cumin.
5. Now take the chicken roll-ups and dip each one in flour, then melted butter, then the crumb mixture.
6. Place seam-side down in a single layer in greased slow cooker.
7. Cook on Low for 4–4½ hours, until chicken registers 165° on a meat thermometer.
8. Gently transfer chicken rolls to a rimmed baking sheet. Place them under a broiler until crumbs are crispy and slightly browned. Watch carefully!
9. Be sure to remove toothpicks before serving or else give your diners a heads-up.

Why I like this recipe —
I love the juicy chicken which benefits from the slow cooker's moist heat in contrast to the crispy crumbs on top. We especially like these in summer with corn on the cob on the side.

Italian Chicken Fajita Wraps

Makes 4-6 servings

Prep. Time: 20 minutes ❧ Cooking Time: 2-4 hours ❧ Chilling Time: 4-8 hours or overnight
Ideal slow-cooker size: 3-quart

1 lb. boneless, skinless chicken breasts

2 garlic cloves, sliced thinly

2 Tbsp. dried oregano

1 Tbsp. dried parsley

1 tsp. dried basil

½ tsp. dried thyme

¼ tsp. celery seed

1 Tbsp. sugar

½ tsp. salt

1 tsp. freshly ground pepper

8-oz. bottle Italian salad dressing

1 cup salsa

1 green bell pepper, sliced in ribs

1 red bell pepper, sliced in ribs

1 medium onion, sliced in rings

10 10"-flour tortillas

TOPPINGS, CHOOSE ALL OR SOME:

freshly grated Parmesan cheese

fresh mozzarella slices

hot sauce, *or* pickled Italian hot peppers

chopped olives

lemon wedges

shredded lettuce

chopped tomatoes

chopped fresh basil

1. Cut chicken into thin strips. Place in large mixing bowl.

2. Add garlic, herbs, sugar, salt, pepper, salad dressing, and salsa. Mix well. Cover and marinate 4–8 hours or overnight in the fridge.

3. Pour chicken and marinade into slow cooker. Cook on Low for 2–4 hours, until chicken is white through the middle and tender.

4. Spoon the chicken with its sauce into an oven-proof serving dish or rimmed baking sheet. Add the vegetables. Slide it under the broiler for a few minutes until browned spots appear on the chicken and vegetables.

5. Serve with tortillas and toppings and lots of napkins.

Why I like this recipe —
   These wraps are always a crowd-pleaser because they're so customizable. However, they are quite messy, so sometimes I skip the tortillas and serve the warm chicken over a bed of salad greens with Italian bread on the side.

QUICK *and* EASY

Turkey with Mushroom Sauce

Makes 12 servings
Prep. Time: 15 minutes ❦ *Cooking Time: 4½ hours*
Ideal slow-cooker size: 3-quart

2 lbs. boneless skinless turkey thighs, cut in 2" chunks

1 medium onion, chopped

3 cups sliced mushrooms

3 Tbsp. butter

2 Tbsp. soy sauce

★ ½ cup beef stock

1 tsp. poultry seasoning

¼ cup all-purpose flour

½ cup water

¼ cup chopped fresh parsley

★ TO MAKE YOUR OWN STOCK, SEE PAGE 357.

1. Place turkey, onions, mushrooms, butter, soy sauce, stock, and poultry seasoning in slow cooker.

2. Cover and cook on Low for 4 hours.

3. Whisk together flour and water until smooth. Pour into hot mixture in slow cooker, stirring continuously until blended. A small whisk will work for this.

4. Cover and cook an additional 30 minutes on Low, until sauce is thickened and hot. Check flavor and add a bit more poultry seasoning or salt if needed.

5. Garnish with parsley. Serve over broad egg noodles or next to a rice pilaf.

King Turkey

Makes 10-12 servings
Prep. Time: 20 minutes ❧ *Cooking Time: 5-7 hours*
Ideal slow-cooker size: 4- or 5-quart

5- to 6-lb. turkey breast,
bone in and skin on

1 medium onion, chopped

1 rib celery, chopped

half stick (¼ cup) melted butter

a good shower of salt to taste

a sprinkling of lemon pepper to taste

★ 1 cup chicken broth

1 cup white wine

★ TO MAKE YOUR OWN BROTH, SEE PAGE 357

1. Wash turkey breast. Pat dry. Put onion and celery in cavity. Place in greased slow cooker.

2. Pour melted butter over turkey. Season with salt and lemon pepper.

3. Pour broth and wine around turkey.

4. Cover. Cook on Low 5-7 hours, or just until meat thermometer registers 165°. (Make sure thermometer does not touch the bone.)

5. Let stand 15 minutes before carving.

Turkey Barbecue

Makes 10 sandwiches
Prep. Time: 20 minutes ❦ Cooking Time: 7-9 hours
Ideal slow-cooker size: 6-quart

4- or 5-lb. turkey breast
with the bone in

olive oil

1-2 Tbsp. water

BARBECUE SAUCE:

3 Tbsp. butter

1 chopped onion

1 cup chicken broth

½-1 cup ketchup

1 tsp. salt

dash pepper

2 Tbsp. apple cider vinegar

4-6 Tbsp. brown sugar

1 Tbsp. prepared mustard

1-2 Tbsp. Worcestershire sauce

a few dashes of hot sauce

1. Rub the breast inside and out with olive oil.

2. Put the breast into your slow cooker.

3. Add the water.

4. Cover. Cook on Low 5-6 hours, or until the meat registers 165° in the center of the breast (but not touching the bone) on a quick-read thermometer.

5. Lift breast out of the cooker and let it cool. Then debone it. Cube the meat or shred it with two forks.

6. Use 1 cup of the broth in the Barbecue Sauce. Freeze the rest of the broth and use it to make soup or rice. Mix all ingredients for the Barbecue Sauce.

7. Put the meat back into the cooker.

8. Pour the sauce over the cut-up turkey and mix everything together well.

9. Cover. Heat on Low 2-3 hours, or until it's heated through. Then serve it on sandwich rolls that are sturdy enough to handle the sauce.

Why I like this recipe —
    I first ate this at a baby shower. Suddenly it was more interesting than the baby gifts. Or the cupcakes. Don't forget this recipe when you're hosting any kind of event. Serve it on little party rolls or on big and beefy Kaisers.

Creamy Turkey with Vegetables Dinner

Makes 4-6 servings
Prep. Time: 15 minutes ❧ Cooking Time: 4-5 hours
Ideal slow-cooker size: 5-quart

1 onion, diced

6 small red potatoes, quartered

2 cups sliced carrots

2 lbs. boneless, skinless turkey thighs, cut into 4-6 pieces

¼ cup flour

2 Tbsp. (1 envelope) dry onion soup mix

½ tsp. dried sage

½ tsp. dried thyme

★ 10¾-oz. can cream of mushroom soup

★★ ⅔ cup chicken broth, *or* water

★ TO MAKE YOUR OWN CREAM SOUP, SEE PAGES 370-371.
★★ TO MAKE YOUR OWN BROTH, SEE PAGE 357.

1. Place vegetables in bottom of slow cooker.
2. Place turkey thighs over vegetables.
3. Combine remaining ingredients. Pour over turkey.
4. Cover and cook on Low 4–5 hours.

Why I like this recipe —
This is sturdy and satisfying.
You won't find anyone who's eaten
it showing up in the kitchen an
hour later, huntin' a snack.

Barbecued Turkey Cutlets (with a great variation)

Makes 6-8 servings
Prep. Time: 10 minutes   Cooking Time: 4 hours
Ideal slow-cooker size: 4- or 5-quart

6-8 (1½-2 lbs.) turkey cutlets
¼ cup molasses
¼ cup apple cider vinegar
½ cup ketchup
3 Tbsp. Worcestershire sauce
1 tsp. garlic salt
3 Tbsp. chopped onion
2 Tbsp. brown sugar
¼-½ tsp. pepper

1. Place turkey cutlets in slow cooker.
2. Combine remaining ingredients in a bowl. Pour over turkey.
3. Cover. Cook on Low 4 hours. Serve over white or brown rice.

A great variation—

You can use this same sauce to make Barbecued Turkey Legs. Put 4 drumsticks into a slow cooker. Top with the sauce. Cook on Low 5-7 hours, or until the meat is tender but not dry. These go well with white or brown rice, too.

Hot Turkey Salad

Makes 8 servings

Prep. Time: 20-30 minutes • Cooking Time: 2¾-3¼ hours

Ideal slow-cooker size: 4-quart

4 cups cooked, cubed turkey

4 cups celery, chopped
(get out your food processor)

1 cup blanched almonds, chopped

¾ cup chopped green bell pepper

¼ cup chopped pimento

¼ cup chopped onion

2 tsp. salt

¼ cup lemon juice

1 cup mayonnaise

8 oz. Swiss cheese, sliced

1 stick (½ cup) butter, melted

2 cups cracker crumbs

1. If you don't have cooked turkey (or chicken), flip to page 360 for a recipe for cooking poultry in your slow cooker, so you have it ready for recipes like this one. If you've got the cooked turkey already, go ahead with Step 2.

2. In a big bowl, gently mix together the turkey, celery, almonds, green pepper, pimentos, onion, salt, lemon juice, and mayonnaise.

3. Spoon the mixture into your greased slow cooker. Top with slices of cheese.

4. Cover. Cook on Low 2½-3 hours, or until the celery, pepper, and onions are as tender as you like them.

5. While the turkey is cooking, combine the melted butter and cracker crumbs in a small bowl.

6. When the turkey is finished cooking, sprinkle the buttered cracker crumbs over top.

7. Continue cooking, uncovered, for 15 minutes, or until the topping is heated through.

Why I like this recipe—

This recipe flirts with being a salad. I love the crunch throughout and on top, so I go for the shorter cooking time. But, hey, it's your meal, so cook it as long as you want. No right or wrong here.

Turkey Enchiladas

Makes 6 servings
Prep. Time: 20-30 minutes ❦ Cooking Time: 4-6 hours
Ideal slow-cooker size: 4-quart

1 large onion, chopped

2 Tbsp. olive oil

¼ tsp. garlic powder

1 tsp. salt

½ tsp. dried oregano

2 4-oz. cans diced green chilies

28-oz. can stewed tomatoes

6 corn, *or flour*, tortillas, *divided*

2 cups chopped, cooked turkey

1 cup sour cream, plus more for passing as a topping

2 cups grated cheddar cheese, plus more for passing as a topping

fresh cilantro, chopped, for topping

*Why I like this recipe —
A good, messy Mexican
staple. You'll hear
"Make this again!"*

1. Saute the onion in the olive oil in a good-sized skillet. When the onion softens, stir in the garlic powder, salt, and oregano. Give the mixture a swirl, and then take it off the heat.

2. Stir in the chilies and tomatoes.

3. Lay 2 tortillas into the bottom of your greased slow cooker. Tear them so that they cover the bottom of the cooker as much as possible.

4. Ladle in ⅓ of the tomato mixture.

5. Mix the turkey, 1 cup sour cream, and 2 cups grated cheese together in a bowl. Spoon ⅓ of that mixture over the tomato sauce.

6. Repeat the layers twice.

7. Cover. Cook on Low 4-6 hours.

8. Let the Enchiladas stand for 15 minutes before serving to let the cheese firm up.

9. Serve with toppings of more sour cream, more grated cheese, and fresh cilantro.

TIP
If you don't have cooked turkey, use chicken, or even hamburger or shredded beef roast.

Main Dishes

Pork

Heritage Pork Roast, page 64

Heritage Pork Roast

Makes 4-6 servings
Prep. Time: 20-30 minutes ❧ Cooking Time: 4-5 hours
Ideal slow-cooker size: 5-quart

½ cup apple juice, *or* apple cider

1½ lbs. sweet potatoes, sliced ½" thick

3 medium onions, peeled, sliced and separated into rings

4 medium apples, sliced

2 lbs. center-cut boneless pork roast, trimmed of fat

2 tsp. Dijon mustard

¼ tsp. black pepper

6 fresh sage leaves, snipped, or ½ tsp. dried sage

¼ cup cold water

1 tsp. brown sugar

2 Tbsp. cornstarch

Why I like this recipe — Years ago butchering was done in the autumn when the sweet potatoes were being dug and the apples were being picked. And so a menu came together. Of course, now we can eat this year-round, and we do.

1. Pour apple juice into slow cooker.

2. Add sweet potatoes slices in a layer, followed by onion rings, and then sliced apples. (I don't peel mine; you certainly can if you want.)

3. In a large nonstick skillet over medium heat, brown pork on all sides.

4. Settle pork onto the apple slices.

5. Brush mustard over the roast. Sprinkle with pepper and sage.

6. Cover and cook on Low 4-5 hours, or until the roast is done and registers 145° on an instant-read thermometer.

7. Move the roast to a platter and cover it with foil to keep it warm.

8. Using a slotted spoon, lift the sweet potato, onion and apple slices into a bowl. Cover to keep the mixture warm.

9. In a small bowl, stir together the water, sugar, and cornstarch until smooth.

10. Stir cornstarch mixture into the juice in the cooker.

11. Cook, stirring often until thickened, about 5-10 minutes.

12. Slice the pork. Top with the sweet potato, onion, and apple slices. Spoon the sauce over everything.

Asian Pork Roast

Makes 4-6 servings
Prep. Time: 15 minutes ❧ Cooking Time: 3-4 hours
Ideal slow-cooker size: 4-quart

¼ cup soy sauce

½ cup ketchup

¼ cup honey

2½- to 3-lb. pork loin

2-3 garlic cloves, sliced

freshly ground black pepper to taste

3 sprigs fresh rosemary, *or* 1 tsp. dried

1. Mix together soy sauce, ketchup, and honey. Set aside.
2. Cut slits into pork loin. Insert slices of garlic into slits. Place pork in slow cooker.
3. Pour soy sauce mixture over pork.
4. Sprinkle pepper over pork. Lay rosemary sprigs on top of roast, or sprinkle with dry rosemary.
5. Cook on Low 3-4 hours, or until meat registers 140-145° on an instant-read thermometer when it's stuck into the center of the roast.
6. Remove to platter and cover with foil to keep warm. Let stand for 10-15 minutes.
7. Slice the meat. Top with soy sauce mixture from the cooker.

TIP

Pork loin can overcook easily, just like chicken breasts. I relaxed a whole lot more about whether a roast was under-done or over-done, once I began using an instant-read meat thermometer.

Cranberry Pork Roast

Makes 6-8 servings

Prep. Time: 20 minutes ❦ *Cooking Time: 4½-5½ hours* ❦ *Standing Time: 25-30 minutes*
Ideal slow-cooker size: 5-quart

2½–3-lb. pork roast

1 tsp. salt

½ tsp. black pepper

1 Tbsp. oil

16-oz. can whole-berry cranberry sauce

½ cup orange juice

¼ cup brown sugar

½ tsp. grated orange peel

pinch ground cloves

1. Pat the roast dry with paper towels. Rub the roast with salt and pepper.
2. Heat the oil in a large skillet and sear the roast on all sides.
3. Combine rest of ingredients in slow cooker.
4. Place seared pork roast in slow cooker and spoon some of the sauce over it.
5. Cover and cook on Low for 4–5 hours, until the roast registers 145° on a meat thermometer.
6. Remove the roast from the pan and place it on a serving platter. Cover with foil and allow to stand for 25-30 minutes to allow the roast to gather its juices and firm up.
7. Slice thinly and serve with the remaining sauce.

Why I like this recipe —
   I love fruit with meat, and I love the flavor of this roast in the middle of winter on one of the holidays. It makes the house smell so good, too!

Sauerkraut and Kielbasa

Makes 6-8 servings
Prep. Time: 20 minutes ❧ Cooking Time: 4-6 hours
Ideal slow-cooker size: 5-quart

5 slices bacon

1 medium
onion, sliced

2 lbs. sauerkraut

1½–2 Tbsp. light
brown sugar

1 lb. kielbasa, cut on
the diagonal into
¾"-thick slices

1. Sauté the bacon in a skillet until it's crisp. Keep the drippings, but remove the bacon and lay it on a paper-towel-covered plate to drain. When it's cool, crumble it coarsely.

2. Saute the onions in the bacon drippings until they're transparent. Remove the onions from the skillet and allow them to drain, too, on a paper-towel-lined plate.

3. Mix the sauerkraut, onion and bacon slices, the brown sugar, and kielbasa slices together in your slow cooker.

4. Cover. Cook on Low for 4-6 hours.

Pork Roast with Sweet Sauerkraut

QUICK
and
EASY

Makes 8 servings
Prep. Time: 15 minutes 🌿 Cooking Time: 5–7 hours
Ideal slow-cooker size: 5-quart

2 3-lb. pork shoulder roasts

27-oz. can sauerkraut

¼ cup brown sugar

2 large apples, peeled or not, and sliced

½ tsp. caraway seeds

1 envelope dry onion soup mix

½ cup water

1. Place roasts in slow cooker.
2. Drain sauerkraut. In a good-sized bowl, combine sauerkraut, brown sugar, apple slices, caraway seeds, and onion soup mix. Layer over roasts. Pour water over all.
3. Cover. Cook on Low 5–7 hours.
4. Lift out roasts and slice or chunk. Place on large platter along with piles of sauerkraut.

Why I like this recipe—
If you're a little wary of sauerkraut, try this slightly sweet version. We call it more-ish. You can barely stop eating once you've started. The caraway seeds elevate the flavor, too. Get your mashed potatoes ready, and you've got a complete meal with very little fuss.

Orchard Ham

Makes 6-8 servings
Prep. Time: 20 minutes & Cooking Time: 8½-10½ hours
Ideal slow-cooker size: 4- or 5-quart

3-lb. ham (or larger; whatever fits your slow cooker)

4 cups cider, *or* apple juice

1 cup brown sugar

2 tsp. dry mustard

1 tsp. ground cloves

1¼ cups golden seedless raisins

TIP

The sliced leftover ham makes great sandwiches.

1. Place ham in slow cooker. Pour cider over meat.

2. Cover. Cook on Low 8-10 hours.

3. While the ham is cooking, make a paste by mixing brown sugar, dry mustard, cloves, and a few tablespoons of hot cider from the cooker in a bowl. Set aside.

4. At the end of the cooking time, remove ham from cider and place in a 9 × 13 baking pan, or one that's big enough to hold the ham.

5. Brush paste over ham. Then pour a cup of juice from the slow cooker into the baking pan. (Don't pour it over the ham; you don't want to wash off the paste.) Stir raisins into the cider in the baking pan.

6. Bake at 375° for 20-30 minutes, or until the paste has turned into a glaze.

7. Let the ham stand for 10-15 minutes, and then slice and serve. Top the slices with the cider-raisin mixture.

Why I like this recipe —
This is special enough for a holiday meal.
But it's simple enough to make anytime.

Balsamic-Glazed Pork Ribs

Makes 6-8 servings

Prep. Time: 30 minutes ❦ *Cooking Time: 4-6 hours* ❦ *Standing Time: 2-12 hours*
Ideal slow-cooker size: 6-quart

2 Tbsp. olive oil

½ tsp. dried rosemary

1 Tbsp. kosher salt

1 Tbsp. fennel seeds

1 tsp. freshly ground pepper

½ tsp. dried sage

¼ tsp. dried thyme

1 tsp. paprika

pinch–1 tsp. crushed red pepper, depending on the heat you like

½ tsp. ground coriander

¼ tsp. ground allspice

3 lbs. pork ribs

3 Tbsp. balsamic vinegar

1. In a small bowl, combine olive oil, rosemary, salt, fennel seeds, pepper, sage, thyme, paprika, red pepper, coriander, and allspice.

2. Rub spice paste all over ribs and let stand at room temperature for 2 hours, or refrigerate overnight.

3. Place ribs in slow cooker, cutting if needed to fit.

4. Cook on Low for 4-6 hours, until tender.

5. Remove ribs from slow cooker and place on rimmed baking sheet. Preheat broiler. Brush meaty side of ribs with balsamic vinegar and broil 6 inches from heat until browned, about 2 minutes.

6. Let stand for 5 minutes, then cut between ribs, or serve in slabs.

Why I like this recipe —
The flavor combination is delicious. I have read that some people have balsamic vinegar tastings, just the way people taste wine! After enjoying these ribs with their balsamic vinegar, I can understand the attraction.

Tender Zesty Ribs

Makes 4-5 servings
Prep. Time: 20 minutes ❦ Cooking Time: 4-6 hours
Ideal slow-cooker size: 5-quart

4 lbs. pork spareribs, *or* country-style ribs

1–2 Tbsp. oil

1½ cups apple cider vinegar

1 cup ketchup

¼ cup sugar

¼ cup Worcestershire sauce

2 cloves garlic, minced

2 tsp. ground mustard

2 tsp. paprika

1–1½ tsp. salt

¼ tsp. pepper

1. Cut ribs into serving-size pieces. Brown tops and bottoms in oil in a large skillet.

2. Combine rest of the ingredients in a slow cooker. Put ribs into slow cooker, submerging the ribs in the sauce.

3. Cover. Cook on Low 4–6 hours, or until the meat is tender and starting to fall off the bones.

4. Lift ribs onto a platter. Spoon sauce over top. Pass any remaining sauce in a small bowl.

Why I like this recipe —
    You've got all of these sauce ingredients in your pantry already. So add the ribs to your next grocery list. This is a wow recipe with a little sting.

Our Favorite *Ribs*

Makes 4 servings
Prep. Time: 20 minutes ❦ Cooking Time: 3½–4½ hours
Ideal slow-cooker size: 4- or 5-quart

2 Tbsp. oil

2 lbs. pork spareribs, cut in pieces

¼ cup chopped onion

¼ cup chopped green bell pepper

1 cup crushed pineapple, undrained

¾ cup vinegar

¾ cup water, *divided*

2 Tbsp. ketchup

½ cup brown sugar

2 Tbsp. soy sauce

1 tsp. Worcestershire sauce

2 cloves garlic, sliced thinly

2 Tbsp. cornstarch

1. Brown spareribs in oil in large skillet. Remove meat and place in slow cooker.
2. Pour off all but 2 Tbsp. drippings from the skillet.
3. Add onion and green pepper and cook until tender. Stir in pineapple, vinegar, ½ cup water, ketchup, brown sugar, soy sauce, Worcestershire sauce, and garlic. Bring to boil.
4. Pour hot sauce over spareribs in slow cooker.
5. Cover and cook on Low for 3-4 hours, until ribs are falling-off-the-bone tender.
6. Whisk together the remaining ¼ cup water with the cornstarch. Whisk into sauce and ribs in slow cooker. Cover and cook on Low for an additional 10–20 minutes, until thickened.

Pork Chops Deluxe

Makes 6 servings

Prep. Time: 25 minutes ✿ *Cooking Time: 4½ hours*

Ideal slow-cooker size: 5-quart

2 Tbsp. oil

2 medium onions, sliced

¼ cup all-purpose flour

1 tsp. garlic powder

1 tsp. coarse (kosher) salt

1 tsp. black pepper

1 tsp. dried basil

6 6-oz. bone-in blade pork chops, ¾" thick

1 cup burgundy wine

★ 14½-oz. can, *or* 1¾ cups, beef broth

1 broth can filled with water, *or* 1¾ cups water

6-oz. can tomato sauce

8 ozs. dried apricots

½ lb. fresh mushroom caps

★ TO MAKE YOUR OWN STOCK, SEE PAGE 357.

Why I like this recipe — I made this for my mom on her birthday. She's a pork-chop lover, and this exceeded her standard.

1. Saute onions in oil in medium-hot, large skillet. Stir frequently.

2. When softened, spoon onions into slow cooker. Reserve drippings in skillet.

3. Meanwhile, place flour, garlic powder, salt, pepper, and basil in strong plastic bag. Squeeze to mix well.

4. One at a time, put chops in bag. Shake well to coat with seasoned flour.

5. As you finish coating each chop, add to the hot skillet and brown quickly on top and bottom. (Rather than crowd the skillet, do the browning in batches. Otherwise, the chops will steam in each other's juices instead of browning quickly.)

6. Pour any extra seasoned flour over the chops in the skillet.

7. In large bowl mix together wine, broth, water, and tomato sauce, then pour over meat. Bring to a boil.

8. Remove chops from skillet and place in cooker. Top with apricots and mushrooms. Pour broth over top.

9. Cover. Cook on Low for 2½ hours. Then cook on High for 1½ hours.

Pork Chop and Rice Bake

Makes 4-6 servings
Prep. Time: 20 minutes ✻ Cooking Time: 2-7 hours
Ideal slow-cooker size: 4- or 5-quart

4-6 ¾"-thick, blade pork chops

3 cups water

½ cup white long-grain rice, uncooked

½ cup brown long-grain rice, uncooked

★ 10¾-oz. can cream of mushroom soup

1 tsp. salt

¼ tsp. pepper

1 Tbsp. chopped fresh parsley, or 1 tsp. dried, optional

★ TO MAKE YOUR OWN CREAM SOUP, SEE PAGES 370-371.

1. Rub skillet with fatty side of pork chop. Saute chops in skillet until brown. Don't crowd the skillet, or they'll just steam rather than browning. So do them in batches. Flip over when the first side is browned and brown the other side. Transfer to the slow cooker.

2. While the chops are browning, mix the water, rice, mushroom soup, salt, and pepper together in a good-sized bowl. Pour over chops when you've put them in the cooker.

3. Cover. Cook on Low 5-7 hours, or on High 2-3 hours.

4. Sprinkle with parsley just before serving if you wish.

TIP

Don't skip the browning step. But if you try to squeeze too many chops in the pan at once, it's not worth the effort. They'll just steam in each other's juices.

Rosemary Pork Loin

Makes 8-10 servings

Prep. Time: 5-10 minutes ❧ *Cooking Time: 4 hours* ❧ *Chilling Time: 8 hours or overnight*
Ideal slow-cooker size: 5-quart

4- *or* 5-lb. pork loin

2 cups apple cider

2 cloves garlic, minced

1 tsp. onion salt

¾ tsp. chopped fresh oregano, *or* ¼ tsp. dried

1 Tbsp. fresh rosemary leaves, *or* 1 tsp. dried

1 bay leaf

1. Place roast in baking pan.
2. Mix together remaining ingredients in a bowl. Pour over roast.
3. Cover. Refrigerate for at least 8 hours. When you think of it, spoon some of the marinade over the roast.
4. Place roast in slow cooker. Pour marinade over roast.
5. Cover. Cook on Low 3½–4 hours, or until meat registers 140-145° on an instant-read thermometer when it's stuck into the center of the roast.
6. When the meat is finished cooking, lift out of cooker onto a platter. Cover with foil to keep it warm. Let stand 15 minutes before slicing.
7. Slice and serve topped with marinade. (Fish out the bay leaf before serving.)

Why I like this recipe—
Squash is such a neutral, yet creamy ingredient. I like its quiet manners next to the bolder apples and seasonings in this dish.

Autumn Harvest Pork Loin

Makes 4-6 servings

Prep. Time: 30 minutes ❧ Cooking Time: 4½-5½ hours ❧ Standing Time: 10-15 minutes
Ideal slow-cooker size: 5-quart

1½ whole butternut squashes, peeled and cubed

1 cup cider, *or* apple juice

2-lb. pork loin

salt

pepper

2 large Granny Smith apples, peeled and quartered

⅓ cup brown sugar

¼ tsp. cinnamon

¼ tsp. dried thyme

¼ tsp. dried sage

TIP
Don't overcook the pork. Think of it as being as delicate as chicken breasts or white fish. Treat it nicely.

1. Put peeled and cubed squash into slow cooker. Pour in cider. Cover and cook on Low 1½ hours.

2. Sprinkle pork loin with salt and pepper on all sides. Settle into slow cooker on top of the squash.

3. Lay apple quarters around the meat.

4. Sprinkle everything with brown sugar, cinnamon, thyme, and sage.

5. Cover. Cook on Low 3-4 hours. Stick your instant-read thermometer into the center of the loin. The meat is done the minute the thermometer reads 140°.

6. Remove pork from cooker. Cover with foil to keep warm. Continue cooking the squash and apples if they're not as tender as you like them.

7. You can cut the loin into ½"-thick slices after it's stood 10-15 minutes. Keep covered until ready to serve.

8. Serve topped with apples and squash. Pass the cooking juices in a small bowl to spoon over the meat, squash, and apples.

Pork Loin with Fruit Stuffing

Makes 10-12 servings

Prep. Time: 30 minutes ❦ *Soaking Time: 1 hour* ❦ *Cooking Time: 4 hours*
Ideal slow-cooker size: 6-quart

1 cup dried apricots, finely chopped

2 Tbsp. brandy, *or* apple juice

6 strips bacon

1 medium onion, finely chopped

2 cups bread crumbs

1 cup chicken broth

4- to 5-lb. boneless pork loin, a short and wide one so it fits in your slow cooker

salt and pepper

TIP

If it's convenient, you can make this a day ahead of when you want to serve it. The roast improves in flavor and texture if it's been made ahead of time and chilled before you slice it. You can serve it cold or re-heated.

1. Soak apricots in brandy or apple juice for 1 hour. They should absorb most or all of the liquid.

2. In the meantime fry bacon strips in a skillet. Reserve the drippings, but lift the bacon out onto a paper-towel-lined plate to drain. When the bacon has cooled, snap it into small pieces.

3. Sauté the chopped onion in the bacon drippings.

4. In a medium bowl, combine the softened onion with the drained apricots, bacon pieces, bread crumbs, and chicken broth to make the fruit stuffing.

5. Slice the pork loin lengthwise, but stop just before cutting through the other long side. You should be able to open the loin and lay it flat.

6. Spread the stuffing along the inside of pork. Then roll it snugly, starting from the one long side. Keep tucking in the stuffing as you roll. Tie the roll securely with kitchen twine in 3 or 4 places to hold it shut.

7. Put the stuffed loin into your greased slow cooker, fat side up. Sprinkle it generously with salt and pepper.

8. Cover the cooker. Cook the meat on Low about 4 hours, or until your instant-read meat thermometer registers 140-145° when stuck into the center of the meat.

9. Let the meat stand for about 10 minutes before cutting the twine and removing it. Then slice the stuffed meat and serve.

Garage Sale Stew

Makes 6-8 servings
Prep. Time: 30 minutes 🌼 Cooking Time: 2-4 hours
Ideal slow-cooker size: 6-quart

2-3 Tbsp. olive oil

1 lb. sausage—your choice of flavors—links, *or* casings removed and meat crumbled

1 large onion, chopped

10-oz. can tomatoes with green chili peppers

1 Tbsp. Worcestershire sauce

1½ tsp. dry mustard

¼ cup honey

1-lb. can lima, *or* butter beans, drained, with liquid reserved

1-lb. can red kidney beans, drained, with liquid reserved

1-lb. can garbanzo beans, drained, with liquid reserved

1. Place oil in a large skillet. Brown the sausage in the oil. Using a slotted spoon, lift the crumbled sausage into the slow cooker. If you're using links, lift them out of the cooker with a slotted spoon and let them cool until you can stand to hold them. Then cut them into thin slices and put them in the cooker.

2. Brown the onion in the drippings in the skillet. Add them to the cooker.

3. Stir the tomatoes and peppers into the skillet. Heat them up, and then stir loose any brown bits stuck on the bottom of the skillet. The acid in the tomatoes will help to lift the bits so you can add them to the slow cooker, too. Pour the tomatoes-drippings mixture into the cooker.

4. Add everything else and stir well. Mix in the reserved juice from the lima, kidney, and garbanzo beans if there's enough room in the cooker.

5. Cover. Cook on Low 2-4 hours. This holds well on Warm if you aren't ready to eat at the end of the cooking time.

Why I like this recipe —
   This is the story: My friend mixed up this stew the night before her garage sale. Early in the morning, she plugged it in in a corner of her garage. All morning long, people commented on the delicious smell, and she ended up giving away most of the stew as samples in paper cups! Talk about community spirit!

Kielbasa and Cheese Pasta Sauce

Makes 4-5 servings
Prep. Time: 20 minutes ❦ *Cooking Time: 6-8 hours*
Ideal slow-cooker size: 4-quart

★ 1 cup beef stock

¼ cup all-purpose flour

2 Tbsp. butter, melted

4 oz. cheese, of your choice, shredded

1 lb. kielbasa, sliced

1 small onion, chopped

2 ribs celery, diced

2 carrots, grated

2-oz. jar pimentos

12-oz. box pasta, of your choice

★ TO MAKE YOUR OWN STOCK, SEE PAGE 357

1. Heat beef stock in microwave or on stove-top until boiling.

2. Add the boiling stock to slow cooker. Add rest of ingredients, except for the pasta, stirring gently until well mixed.

3. Cover. Cook on Low 6–8 hours, or until vegetables are as soft as you like them.

4. As you near the end of the cooking time, cook pasta on the stove-top. Drain and keep warm.

5. Mix the finished sauce with the pasta.

Cozy Kielbasa

Makes 6 servings
Prep. Time: 20 minutes ♈ Cooking Time: 4 hours
Ideal slow-cooker size: 5-quart

2 lbs. smoked kielbasa

★ **1¾ cups unsweetened
applesauce**

¼ cup brown sugar

3 medium onions, sliced

★ TO MAKE YOUR OWN APPLESAUCE, SEE PAGE 367

1. Slice kielbasa into ¼" slices. Brown in skillet. Stir often to make sure all sides brown. Drain the kielbasa of any drippings.

2. Combine applesauce and brown sugar in slow cooker.

3. Stir in the kielbasa and onions.

4. Cover. Cook on Low 4 hours.

Sausage Sweet Potato Bake

Makes 4-6 servings
Prep. Time: 30 minutes 🍃 Cooking Time: 4-6 hours
Ideal slow-cooker size: 4-quart

1 lb. bulk, *or* **link, sausage**

2 medium raw sweet potatoes, peeled *or* **not**

3 medium apples, peeled *or* **not**

2 Tbsp. brown sugar

1 Tbsp. flour

¼ tsp. salt

½ cup water

1. If you can't find bulk sausage, just buy links and squeeze it out of the casing. Brown the sausage in a skillet, breaking it up into small clumps as it cooks. Drain off the drippings.
2. If you're peeling the potatoes and apples, now's the time to do that.
3. Layer the sausage, then the sweet potatoes, and finally the apples into your greased slow cooker.
4. In a small bowl, combine all the other ingredients until smooth. Pour the sauce over the layers.
5. Cover. Cook on Low 4-6 hours, or until the sweet potatoes are as tender as you like them.

Ham Balls and Sauce

Makes 30 meatballs
Prep. Time: 20-30 minutes ❦ Cooking Time: 4-6 hours
Ideal slow-cooker size: 5-quart

HAM BALLS:

1 lb. ground ham

1½ lbs. ground pork

2 cups bread crumbs

2 eggs

1 cup milk

SAUCE:

¾ cup brown sugar

1 tsp. prepared mustard

½ tsp. paprika

¼ cup vinegar

4 oz. pineapple chunks

1. In a good-sized bowl, combine all ham ball ingredients. Shape into 30 balls. Stack the ham balls into your greased slow cooker.

2. Stir all of the sauce ingredients together. Pour the sauce over the ham balls.

3. Cover. Cook on Low 4-6 hours, or until the meatballs are tender. If you wish, you may gently stir at the 4-hour mark to put the topmost ham balls down into the sauce.

4. Move the balls onto a rimmed platter and spoon the sauce over top before serving. Lovely served over rice.

Here's a different sauce you can try —

10¾-oz. can tomato soup

½ cup water

½ cup vinegar

1 cup brown sugar

1 tsp. prepared mustard

Why I like this recipe —
This was my mother-in-law's main dish when she still cooked a full Christmas for her tribe of kids and grandkids. Now that my generation cooks the holiday meals, we often still make this. But it's a great anytime-meal. Ask the butcher to grind the ham and pork if you don't see it at your meat counter.

Sweet Potatoes, Ham, and Oranges

Makes 4 servings
Prep. Time: 15 minutes   Cooking Time: 4–5 hours
Ideal slow-cooker size: 3- or 4-quart

2–3 raw sweet potatoes,
peeled and sliced ¼" thick

1 large ham slice, cut into 4 pieces

3 seedless oranges, peeled and sliced

3 Tbsp. orange juice concentrate

3 Tbsp. honey

¼ tsp. ground allspice

⅛ tsp. pepper

½ cup brown sugar

1 Tbsp. cornstarch

TIP
Be sure to use
orange juice
concentrate, rather
than juice, for the
best flavor.

1. Place sweet potatoes in slow cooker.

2. Arrange ham and orange slices on top.

3. Combine remaining ingredients. Drizzle over ham and oranges.

4. Cover. Cook on Low 4–5 hours, or just until the sweet potatoes are as tender as you like them.

Brats and Spuds

Makes 6 servings

Prep. Time: 35 minutes ✂ Cooking Time: 5-6 hours

Ideal slow-cooker size: 4-quart

1–2 Tbsp. oil

5–6 bratwurst links, cut into 1″ pieces

5 medium-sized potatoes, peeled and cubed

27-oz. can sauerkraut, rinsed and drained

1 medium tart apple, chopped

1 small onion, chopped

⅓–½ cup packed brown sugar

½ tsp. salt

1. Brown bratwurst in oil on all sides in a skillet.

2. Combine remaining ingredients in a slow cooker.
   Stir in bratwurst and pan drippings.

3. Cover. Cook on Low 5-6 hours, or until potatoes and apples are tender.

TIP

Not sure about bratwurst? Switch in Italian sausage if you want—sweet or hot.

Slurping Good Sausages

Makes 6-8 servings
Prep. Time: 20 minutes   ❦   Cooking Time: 6 hours
Ideal slow-cooker size: 4-quart

2 lbs. sweet Italian sausage, cut into 5" lengths

24-oz. jar of your favorite pasta sauce

6-oz. can tomato paste

1 large green pepper, chopped

1 large onion, sliced thin

1 Tbsp. grated Parmesan cheese, plus a little more

1 cup water

2 Tbsp. chopped fresh parsley, *or* 2 tsp. dried parsley

1. Place sausage pieces in skillet. Add water to cover. Simmer 10 minutes. Drain. (This cooks off some of the fat from the sausage.)

2. Combine pasta sauce, tomato paste, chopped green pepper, sliced onion, 1 Tbsp. grated cheese, and water in slow cooker. Stir in sausage pieces.

3. Cover. Cook on Low 6 hours.

4. Just before serving, stir in parsley.

5. Serve in buns, or cut sausage into bite-sized pieces and serve over cooked pasta. Sprinkle with more Parmesan cheese.

Why I like this recipe —
When you're tired or can't think anymore, this is the dish to make. It bucks everyone up, it's so satisfyingly good. I love its versatility, too. Buns or pasta. Or rice or potatoes.

Creamy Ham and Scalloped Potatoes

Makes 12 servings

Prep. Time: 30-40 minutes ❦ *Cooking Time: 6-8 hours*

Ideal slow-cooker size: 5-quart

6–8 slices ham, cut ¼"
thick, cubed, *divided*

8–10 medium potatoes, peeled
and thinly sliced, *divided*

1 large onion, sliced, *divided*

salt and pepper to taste, *divided*

1 cup grated cheddar cheese, *divided*

★ 10½-oz. can cream of
mushroom soup

paprika

★ TO MAKE YOUR OWN CREAM SOUP, SEE PAGES 370-371.

1. Put half of the ham, half of the potatoes and half of the onion into your greased slow cooker.

2. Sprinkle with salt, pepper and half the grated cheese. Repeat the same layers in the same order.

3. Pour the soup into a bowl and stir it briskly until it gets all creamy and saucy. Then spoon it over top of the ingredients in the cooker.

4. Cover and cook on Low 6-8 hours, or until the potatoes and onions are as tender as you like them.

5. Just before serving, sprinkle with paprika.

Why I like this recipe —
   This is an old classic. But I hardly ever made it, because I'm too impatient to slice this many potatoes thin. I skipped peeling the potatoes (after cooking them for 6-8 hours, no one ever notices the peels), but the endless slicing still tripped me up. Until I got a mandolin. Now I zip through the potatoes— yes, using the guard faithfully! It's a welcome-home dish.

Sausage Baked Corn

Makes 6 servings
Prep. Time: 15 minutes   Cooking Time: 3-3½ hours
Ideal slow-cooker size: 4-quart

1 lb. bulk pork sausage

¼ cup chopped onion

1 tsp. salt

1 quart frozen, *or* fresh corn, thawed and drained

1 cup soft bread crumbs

4 eggs, well beaten

½ cup ketchup

⅛ tsp. ground allspice

pinch cayenne

1. In a skillet, fry together sausage, onion, and salt until sausage is mostly browned. Discard drippings.

2. In a mixing bowl, combine sausage, onions, corn, and bread crumbs. Mix well.

3. The mixture should be cool enough to add eggs without scrambling them on contact. If not, stir and spread out the mixture in the bowl until it is just warm. Add eggs and stir again.

4. Pour mixture into lightly greased slow cooker.

5. In a small bowl, mix ketchup with allspice and cayenne.

6. Spread ketchup mixture over corn and sausage mixture.

7. Cover and cook on Low for 3-3½ hours, until set in the middle.

Pork Barbecue Sandwiches

Makes 8 servings
Prep. Time: 15-20 minutes   Cooking Time: 5-6 hours
Ideal slow-cooker size: 4-quart

3- to 4-lb. boneless pork loin roast

1½ tsp. seasoned salt

1 tsp. garlic powder

dash of pepper

1 cup barbecue sauce, your choice

1 cup cola, regular *or* diet

1. Cut the roast in half. Place both halves in your slow cooker.
2. Sprinkle with salt, garlic powder, and pepper.
3. Cover. Cook 4 hours on Low.
4. Put the cooked meat on a good-sized platter. Skim the fat from the broth remaining in the slow cooker and discard it.
5. Shred the pork using 2 forks. Return the shredded pork to the broth in the slow cooker.
6. Combine the barbecue sauce and cola in a small bowl. Stir it into the meat in the cooker.
7. Cover. Cook on High 1-2 hours, or until the meat's heated through and bubbly.
8. Serve it on rolls.

Main Dishes

Beef

Deep, Dark, and Delicious
Barbecue Sandwiches, page 116

Ginger Pot Roast

Makes 6 servings

Prep. Time: 20 minutes   Cooking Time: 8-10 hours

Ideal slow-cooker size: 4-quart

3-lb. boneless beef pot roast

2 Tbsp. flour

1 Tbsp. oil

2 large onions, chopped

½ tsp. salt, *or* to taste

¼ tsp. black pepper

½ cup soy sauce

1 cup water

2" piece ginger root, diced, no need to peel

½ tsp. ground ginger

2 spring onions, chopped

1. Dip roast in flour and brown on all sides in oil in skillet. Remove roast from skillet and set aside.

2. Cook chopped onions in oil and browned bits left in skillet until just tender. Use a wooden spoon to stir onions and loosen browned bits from pan.

3. Stir in salt and pepper.

4. Spoon onion mixture into slow cooker. Settle roast on top of onions.

5. Combine soy sauce, water, and chopped ginger. Pour over meat.

6. Cover. Cook on Low 8-10 hours.

7. Stir ground ginger and spring onions into liquid. Taste to correct seasonings. Slice roast and serve over rice, mashed potatoes, or your favorite stir-fried vegetables and noodles.

TIP

Leftovers, if there are any, make perfect sandwiches.

Alpine Beef

Makes 6 servings
Prep. Time: 25 minutes ❧ Cooking Time: 6½–7½ hours
Ideal slow-cooker size: 5-quart

3- to 3½-lb. boneless beef chuck roast

1–2 Tbsp. oil

3 cups sliced carrots

3 cups sliced onions

2 large kosher dill pickles, chopped

1 cup sliced celery

★ 1½ cups dry red wine, *or* beef broth

⅓ cup German-style, *or* your favorite, prepared mustard

2 tsp. coarsely ground black pepper

2 bay leaves

¼ tsp. ground cloves

⅓ cup flour

★ TO MAKE YOUR OWN BROTH, SEE PAGE 357.

1. Brown the roast on both sides in oil in a skillet.

2. While the meat is browning, prepare the carrots, onions, pickles, and celery. Place in the slow cooker and mix together.

3. Settle roast into cooker on top of the vegetables.

4. In a bowl, mix together the wine, mustard, pepper, bay leaves, and ground cloves. Pour over the meat and vegetables.

5. Cover. Cook on Low 6–7 hours, or until the meat and vegetables are as tender as you like them.

6. Remove meat and vegetables to a large platter. Cover to keep warm.

7. Dip out 1 cup of broth from the cooker. Place in a bowl. Whisk in flour until smooth. Return to cooker. Stir into broth in cooker until smooth.

8. Turn cooker to High and stir, cooking until broth is thickened.

9. Chunk or slice the beef. Return to the slow cooker, along with the vegetables until hot.

10. Serve over noodles, spaetzle, or mashed potatoes.

Why I like this recipe —
    You eat mustard on your roast beef sandwich, right? So why not slow-cook your roast beef in mustard? You eat relish on your burgers, right? So why not add the "relish"/pickles a little earlier?! The beef responds really well to these extra flavors.

Rich and Tasty Beef Roast

QUICK
and
EASY

Makes 6-8 servings
Prep. Time: 15 minutes   Cooking Time: 5-10 hours
Ideal slow-cooker size: 4- or 5-quart

★ **10¾-oz. can cream of mushroom soup**

3-lb. boneless beef chuck roast

2-3 Tbsp. oil

2 medium onions, sliced thin

3 bay leaves

1 pkg. dry onion soup mix

★ TO MAKE YOUR OWN CREAM SOUP, SEE PAGES 370-371.

1. Spread the mushroom soup in the bottom of a greased slow cooker.
2. Sear the roast on all sides in oil in a hot skillet. Reserve the drippings. Add the browned meat to the slow cooker.
3. Stir the sliced onions into the drippings. Brown, stirring often, to loosen the browned pieces left in the skillet from the meat. When the onions are softened and browned, spread them over the meat.
4. Sprinkle the meat and onions with the dry onion soup mix. Tuck the bay leaves in.
5. Cover and cook on High 5-6 hours, or Low 8-10 hours.
6. Remember to remove the bay leaves before you serve this. Pull the meat apart into great chunks, and then top with the sauce before serving.

Why I like this recipe—
I couldn't resist including this classic slow cooker beef roast recipe. It's so simple, you don't need to think when you make it. It's beloved for a good reason—unforgettable flavor.

Not Just Pot-Roast!

Makes 6-8 servings
Prep. Time: 15 minutes 🌸 Cooking Time: 5½–11½ hours
Ideal slow-cooker size: 5-quart

3- to 3½-lb. boneless chuck roast

2 large onions, sliced

½ cup brown sugar

⅓ cup soy sauce

⅓ cup cider vinegar

2 bay leaves

2–3 garlic cloves, minced

1 tsp. grated fresh ginger

1 cup julienned carrots, matchstick size

2 cups sliced, fresh button mushrooms

2–3 cups fresh spinach leaves, *or* 2 10-oz. pkgs. frozen spinach, thawed and squeezed dry

2 Tbsp. cornstarch

1. Place meat in slow cooker. Spread onion slices over meat.

2. In a bowl, combine brown sugar, soy sauce, vinegar, bay leaves, minced garlic, and grated ginger. Pour over beef and onions.

3. Cover. Cook on High 5–7 hours, or on Low 9–10 hours.

4. Spread carrots, mushrooms, and spinach over beef.

5. Cover. Cook on High 20 minutes.

6. In a small bowl, mix cornstarch with ½ cup broth from slow cooker. Stir back into slow cooker.

7. Cover. Cook 10 minutes more, or until broth thickens.

8. Break beef into chunks. Stir through broth until well mixed. Remove bay leaves.

9. Serve over rice or mashed potatoes.

Why I like this recipe —
I simply love this flavorful meat and broth. Not only that, it is such a good dish to serve to guests because adding the vegetables at the end gives the dish a fresh touch—without panicking the cook.

Slow-Roasted Short Ribs

Makes 12 servings
Prep. Time: 45 minutes   Cooking Time: 9-10 hours
Ideal slow-cooker size: 6-quart

⅔ cup all-purpose flour

1 tsp. salt

½ tsp. pepper

4–4½ lbs. boneless beef short ribs, *or* 6–7 lbs. bone-in beef short ribs

1–2 Tbsp. oil

1–2 Tbsp. butter

1 large onion, chopped

★ 1½ cups beef broth

¾ cup red wine vinegar *or* cider vinegar

½–¾ cup packed brown sugar, depending on how much sweetness you like in a savory dish

½ cup chili sauce

⅓ cup ketchup

⅓ cup Worcestershire sauce

5 garlic cloves, minced

1½ tsp. chili powder

★ TO MAKE YOUR OWN BROTH, SEE PAGE 357.

1. Combine flour, salt, and pepper in a plastic bag. Add ribs, a few at a time, and shake to coat.

2. Melt oil and butter in large skillet.

3. Brown floured meat in batches in skillet, turning to brown each side. Don't crowd the skillet, or the ribs won't brown. They'll just steam in each other's juices.

4. As each rib finishes browning, transfer it into the slow cooker.

5. When all ribs are browned, combine the remaining ingredients in the skillet. Cook, stirring up all the browned drippings left from browning the meat. Cook just until the mixture boils. Pour over the ribs.

6. Cover. Cook on Low 9–10 hours. Let rest for 10 minutes, and then take the bones out.

7. Serve ribs on a platter, topped with the cooking sauce. Pass the rest of the sauce in a small bowl so it can be spooned over the meat and a side dish of rice or noodles.

TIP

If you can, cook these ribs a day before you want to serve them. Cool them down, and then refrigerate them for several hours or overnight. Remove the layer of congealed fat before you serve them.

Braised Beef Short Ribs

Makes 4 servings

Prep. Time: 15 minutes ✻ *Cooking Time: 8-9 hours*

Ideal slow-cooker size: 5-quart

4½ lbs. beef short ribs, ideally 3" long

1½ tsp. kosher (coarse) salt

½ tsp. freshly ground pepper

1½ tsp. dried marjoram, *divided*

14½-oz. can diced tomatoes, including juice

2 Tbsp. balsamic vinegar

2 cups sliced fresh mushrooms

½ cup diced onion

½ cup diced celery

5 garlic cloves, peeled

2 bay leaves

handful chopped fresh parsley, for garnish

1. Sprinkle ribs with salt, pepper, and 1 tsp. marjoram. Pat the seasoning into the meat.

2. Place ribs in slow cooker.

3. Add tomatoes, vinegar, mushrooms, onion, celery, garlic, and bay leaves.

4. Cook on Low for 8-9 hours, until meat is tender.

5. Use a spoon to remove fat off top of sauce if you wish. Remove bay leaves. Stir in remaining ½ tsp. marjoram and taste sauce to see if it needs more salt or pepper.

6. Transfer ribs and sauce to serving bowl and sprinkle with parsley to garnish.

Why I like this recipe — This is a great dish to assemble in the morning (no pre-cooking!) and come home to after a long day away. The excellent flavor is a real welcome home!

Steak Stroganoff

Makes 8 servings
Prep. Time: 15 minutes   ❦   Cooking Time: 6-7 hours
Ideal slow-cooker size: 4-quart

2 Tbsp. flour

½ tsp. black pepper

1 tsp. paprika

½ tsp. garlic salt, *or* seasoning salt

2 lbs. chuck roast, cut into 1½" cubes

★ 10¾-oz. can cream of mushroom soup

½ cup water

1½ Tbsp. Worcestershire sauce

2 cups chopped onions

1 garlic clove, minced

1 cup quartered fresh, small button mushrooms

1 cup sour cream

1 Tbsp. minced fresh parsley

crisp bacon bits, *optional*

cooked, buttered noodles, *or* cooked rice

★ TO MAKE YOUR OWN CREAM SOUP, SEE PAGES 370-371.

1. Combine flour, pepper, paprika, and garlic salt in slow cooker.

2. Place beef cubes in flour mixture and toss until meat is well coated.

3. In a bowl, combine soup, water, Worcestershire sauce, onions, and garlic until well mixed.

4. Pour soupy mixture into slow cooker. Gently stir into beef cubes.

5. Cover. Cook on Low 6-7 hours.

6. Ten minutes before end of cooking time, stir in mushrooms and sour cream. Cover and continue cooking.

7. Serve over hot buttered noodles or cooked rice. Garnish with fresh parsley, and bacon bits, if you wish.

Why I like this recipe—
I grew up eating Beef Stroganoff with ground beef. I've always thought that making the dish with beef cubes is so much more tasty and uptown—if the beef cubes aren't overcooked. Unless you've got a fast and uber-hot slow cooker, this beef is tender but not dry.

Company Stew – At Home or Away

Makes 6-8 servings
Prep. Time: 20 minutes ❦ *Cooking Time: 5-10 hours*
Ideal slow-cooker size: 5-quart

3 thick slices bacon

1 cup flour

½ tsp. salt

¼ tsp. pepper

3- to 3½-lb. boneless chuck roast, cut into 1½" chunks

1 Tbsp. oil, if needed

2 large cloves garlic, sliced thin

1½ cups dry red wine

1½ cups beef broth, or 1½ cups water with 2 beef bouillon cubes

1 large onion, chopped

2 large tomatoes, chopped, or 15½-oz. can stewed tomatoes

1, or 1½, lbs. miniature new potatoes

1¼ tsp. nutmeg

2 tsp. dried thyme

1½ Tbsp. chopped fresh parsley

1. Cut the bacon into pieces. Brown in a skillet. Lift the bacon out with a slotted spoon and let it drain on a paper-towel-covered plate. Keep the drippings in the skillet.

2. Put the flour, salt, and pepper into a sturdy plastic bag. Squish the ingredients around until they're well mixed. Put about ⅓ of the beef cubes into the bag. Tie the bag shut, and then roll the meat around in the dry ingredients.

3. When they're well covered, put them into the hot skillet and brown on all sides.

4. Using the slotted spoon, put the browned beef into the slow cooker.

5. Continue browning the meat, doing half that remains, followed by the rest. Add a Tbsp. of oil to the skillet if the drippings dry up. Continue adding the browned beef to the cooker as it finishes in the skillet.

6. Add all the other ingredients to the cooker, except the parsley and bacon.

7. Cover. Cook on Low 8-10 hours, or on High 5-6 hours.

8. Just before serving, stir in the parsley and bacon.

Why I like this recipe —
    You might think this is only a winter-time dish. But my friend loves it for tailgating parties. Remember—your slow cooker works for you, whether you're eating in or taking the food to a park or parking lot. This will draw a crowd, I promise.

Tender Beef in Wine

QUICK
and
EASY

Makes 10-12 servings
Prep. Time: 20 minutes   Cooking Time: 8-10 hours
Ideal slow-cooker size: 6-quart

6-lb. chuck roast

2 Tbsp. olive oil

1 cup finely chopped celery

1 cup finely chopped onion

½ cup finely chopped mushrooms

12-oz. bottle white cooking wine

1 tsp. dried marjoram

½ tsp. dried rosemary

freshly ground pepper, to taste

1. In large skillet, brown roast on all sides in olive oil.

2. Place roast in slow cooker.

3. Sprinkle chopped celery, onion, and mushrooms over and around roast.

4. Pour white wine over all. Sprinkle marjoram, rosemary, and pepper over meat and vegetables.

5. Cover and cook on Low for 8-10 hours. Roast should be tender and wanting to fall apart.

6. Remove roast from slow cooker and let it stand on a cutting board for 20 minutes before slicing and serving with pan juices.

TIP

Cooking wine is wine with salt added. If you want to use regular drinking wine, you may want to add salt to taste to the dish.

Why I like this recipe—
A tender, luscious roast is just so good. I love to smell this cooking, and I love having the leftovers to put into sandwiches. I really don't see the need to buy lunchmeat when I have such nice slices of beef in the fridge!

Mediterranean Beef

Makes 6-8 servings
Prep. Time: 20 minutes   Cooking Time: 5-7 hours
Ideal slow-cooker size: 4-quart

1 Tbsp. oil

2 lbs. beef, cut
into 2" cubes

4 cups sliced onions

2 tsp. ground coriander

1½ tsp. ground cinnamon

¾ tsp. ground ginger

★ 14½-oz. can beef
broth, plus enough
water to equal 2 cups

1 lb. pitted dried plums

½ tsp. salt

¼ tsp. freshly
ground pepper

juice of one lemon

★ TO MAKE YOUR OWN STOCK, SEE PAGE 357.

1. Brown beef cubes in oil in skillet. Place beef in slow cooker. Reserve drippings.

2. Saute onions in drippings until lightly browned, adding more oil if needed. Using a slotted spoon, lift onions into slow cooker.

3. Stir in remaining ingredients, except lemon juice.

4. Simmer on Low 5-7 hours, adding lemon juice during the last 10 minutes.

*Why I like this recipe —
This is a little taste of
the Mediterranean and
Morocco. It's got a great
sauce, so serve it over rice.*

Burgundy Beef

Makes 6 servings
Prep. Time: 30 minutes ✂ Cooking Time: 4¼–10¼ hours
Ideal slow-cooker size: 3- or 4-quart

2 slices bacon,
cut in squares

¼ cup flour

1 tsp. salt

½ tsp. seasoning salt

¼ tsp. dried marjoram

¼ tsp. dried thyme

¼ tsp. pepper

2 lbs. boneless beef
chuck roast, cut
into 1½" cubes

1 garlic clove, minced

1 beef bouillon
cube, crushed

1 cup burgundy wine

¼ lb. fresh
mushrooms, sliced

1 Tbsp. cornstarch

2 Tbsp. cold water

1. Cook bacon in large skillet until browned and crispy. Remove bacon, reserving drippings.

2. Meanwhile, stir flour, salt, seasoning salt, marjoram, thyme, and pepper together in a bowl. Gently stir in beef cubes until they're all well coated.

3. Brown the meat on all sides in the bacon drippings. Don't crowd the skillet, but do it in batches so the cubes brown and don't just steam in each other's juices.

4. As the meat browns, spoon it into the slow cooker. Mix together whatever flour-y mix remains, along with the minced garlic, beef bouillon, and wine. Stir into meat.

5. Cover. Cook on Low 8–10 hours, or on High 4–5 hours.

6. Stir in mushrooms.

7. In a small bowl, dissolve cornstarch in water. Stir into slow cooker until well blended.

8. Cover. Cook on High 20–30 minutes.

9. Just before serving, stir in crispy bacon. Serve over noodles or mashed potatoes.

TIP

This is an accepting dish. You can add more cut-up vegetables, and you can mix in fresh herbs just before serving.

Why I like this recipe —
The final result tastes like you've labored over it—
but if you can stir, you can make this recipe.

Beef Carbonnade

Makes 10-12 servings
Prep. Time: 20-30 minutes   ❦   Cooking Time: 5-10 hours
Ideal slow-cooker size: 6- or 7-quart

5-lb. boneless beef chuck roast, cut in 1½" cubes

1 cup all-purpose flour, *divided*

4 Tbsp. oil, *divided*

3 cups beer, *divided*

4 medium onions, sliced

6 garlic cloves, crushed

3 Tbsp. brown sugar

1 bay leaf

1 tsp. dried thyme

½ cup chopped parsley

1 Tbsp. salt

2 10½-oz. cans beef consommé

2 Tbsp. red wine vinegar

1 cup cold water

1. Pat beef cubes dry. Put ½ cup flour in large bowl. Add meat to flour and stir until well coated.

2. Put 2 Tbsp. of oil in a large skillet. Add about half the floured meat, or just enough so that the skillet isn't crowded. You want the meat to brown and not just steam in its own juices. Stir to brown on all sides over medium-high heat.

3. When the meat is finished browning, put it into the slow cooker. Continue browning the rest of the meat, adding more oil if needed. Add it to the slow cooker.

4. Pour 1 cup of beer into the skillet. Stir firmly so you lift any browned spots from the skillet into the broth you're creating. Pour into a large bowl. Set aside for a minute.

5. Top the meat with the sliced onions.

6. Add the garlic, brown sugar, bay leaf, thyme, parsley, salt, consommé, the rest of the beer, and wine vinegar to the big bowl with the beer and broth from the skillet. Mix well.

7. Pour mixture over the meat and onions.

8. Cover. Cook on Low for 8-10 hours, or on High 5-6 hours, until meat is tender but not dry.

9. Using a slotted spoon, lift the meat onto a platter. Cover to keep warm.

10. Serve over mashed potatoes, cooked rice, or your favorite pasta. Think about spaetzle…

TO MAKE GRAVY:

11. Cover the cooker. Turn it to High so that the broth simmers.

12. Meanwhile, place remaining ½ **cup flour** into a good-sized jar with a tight-fitting lid. Pour in **1 cup cold water**. Screw the lid on tightly and shake hard until flour and water are well mixed and there are no lumps. Do this off and on for about 5 minutes.

13. When the flour-water mixture is smooth, stir into simmering broth, stirring continually. The broth will thicken slowly. Continue stirring until it's smooth.

14. Pour some of the gravy over the meat. Pour the rest into a bowl and pass along with the meat.

Why I like this recipe —
A couple came up to me a book signing recently, leaned in, and said confidentially, "Guess what the best thing is we make in our slow cooker." I bit. "A chuck roast covered with 3 cans of beer. The beer tenderizes that meat like nothing else we've ever tasted. And we don't even drink!" Try it and see!

Deep, Dark, and Delicious Barbecue Sandwiches

Makes 14-18 servings
Prep. Time: 20-30 minutes (use a food chopper) ❦ *Cooking Time: 5-10 hours*
Ideal slow-cooker size: 5-quart

3 cups chopped celery

1 cup chopped onions

1 cup ketchup

1 cup barbecue sauce

1 cup water

2 Tbsp. vinegar

2 Tbsp. Worcestershire sauce

2 Tbsp. brown sugar

1 tsp. chili powder

1 tsp. salt

½ tsp. pepper

½ tsp. garlic powder

3-4-lb. boneless chuck roast

14-18 hamburger buns

1. Combine all ingredients except roast and buns in slow cooker. When well mixed, put the roast in the cooker. Spoon sauce over top of it.

2. Cover. Cook on High 5-6 hours, or on Low 8-10 hours.

3. Using two forks, pull the meat apart until it's shredded. You can do this in the cooker, or lift it out and do it on a good-sized platter or in a bowl.

4. Stir shredded meat into sauce. Turn the cooker to High if you're ready to eat soon. Or if it will be a while until mealtime, turn the cooker to Low. You're just making sure that the meat and sauce are heated through completely.

5. Serve on buns.

Why I like this recipe—
    You can't beat this for deep, rich flavor. And it's perfect for any occasion with friends and family. I'm not a big fan of cooked celery, so I often up the amount of onions and drop the celery completely. It's that flexible a recipe. Customize it for yourself.

Shredded Taco Beef

Makes 8-10 servings
Prep. Time: 15 minutes ❦ Cooking Time: 8-10 hours
Ideal slow-cooker size: 4-quart

4-lb. boneless beef chuck roast

2 Tbsp. oil

1 tsp. salt

1 tsp. pepper

1 onion, chopped

1 tsp. chili powder

1 tsp. garlic powder

1¼ cups canned diced green chili peppers

½ cup chipotle salsa

¼ cup hot pepper sauce, *or* less if you wish

water

1. Sear roast on all sides in oil in skillet until well browned. Place in slow cooker. Season on all sides with salt and pepper.

2. Mix together the remaining ingredients, except water, in a bowl. Spoon over the meat.

3. Pour the water in along the side of the roast so you don't wash off the topping, until the bottom ⅓ of the roast is covered.

4. Cover. Cook on High 5-6 hours. Reduce to Low and cook 2-4 hours more, just until meat falls apart.

5. If you want a thickened sauce, lift the meat onto a platter using a slotted spoon. Then remove 2 cups broth from the cooker. Stir ¼ cup flour into the hot broth until smooth. Pour the broth back into the cooker, stirring until blended in. Return the meat to the cooker and stir the chunks of meat and sauce together.

Spanish Beef

Makes 10–12 servings
Prep. Time: 10 minutes   Cooking Time: 10–12 hours
Ideal slow-cooker size: 4-quart

1½-lb. boneless beef chuck roast

1 large onion, sliced thin

4-oz. can chopped green chilies, undrained

2 beef bouillon cubes

1½ tsp. dry mustard

½ tsp. garlic powder

1 tsp. seasoning salt

½ tsp. pepper

water

1 cup salsa, as mild or as hot as you like

1. Combine all ingredients except salsa in slow cooker. Add just enough water to cover the meat.

2. Cover cooker and cook on Low 10–12 hours, or until beef is tender but not dry. Lift meat out of cooker into bowl. Reserve liquid in cooker.

3. Shred beef using two forks to pull it apart.

4. Combine beef, salsa and enough of the reserved liquid to have the consistency you want.

5. Use as filling for burritos, chalupas, quesadillas, or tacos.

TIP

You've heard of liquid gold. That's what the broth is that's left in your slow cooker after you've made this Spanish Beef. Use it as a base to make rice. Thicken it with flour as a gravy. Don't pour it away without some serious thought!

Why I like this recipe —
You can't leave this meat alone.
Plus I think it pairs so well with the fresh vegetables, and a spoonful of yogurt on
top that I simply shake my head in wonder. And then I reach for another sandwich.

Middle Eastern Sandwiches
(for a crowd or the freezer)

Makes 10-16 sandwiches
Prep. Time: 50 minutes ❧ Cooking Time: 5-10 hours
Ideal slow-cooker size: 5-quart

4 lbs. boneless beef chuck roast, cut into 1½" cubes

4 Tbsp. cooking oil, *divided*

2 cups chopped onions

2 garlic cloves, minced

1 cup dry red wine

6-oz. can tomato paste

1 tsp. dried oregano

1 tsp. dried basil

½ tsp. dried rosemary

2 tsp. salt

dash of pepper

¼ cup cold water

¼ cup cornstarch

10–16 pita breads

lettuce, tomato, cucumber, and plain yogurt, *optional*, for serving

TIP

Choose whole wheat pitas if you can find them. They're sturdy and less likely to leak than thinner, lighter ones. Plus you get the nutritional benefit.

1. Brown meat, 1 lb. at a time, in skillet in 1 Tbsp. oil. As each pound finishes browning, remove the meat with a slotted spoon and transfer it into the slow cooker. Add more oil as needed with each new pound of beef. Reserve drippings in the skillet.

2. Saute the chopped onions and garlic in drippings until tender.

3. Add wine, tomato paste, oregano, basil, rosemary, salt, and pepper to the onions. Stir, and then spoon over the meat in the cooker.

4. Cover. Cook on Low 8–10 hours, or on High 5–6, or until meat is falling-apart tender, but not dry.

5. Turn cooker to High. Combine cornstarch and water in small bowl until smooth. Stir into meat mixture. Cook until bubbly and thickened, 15–30 minutes, stirring occasionally.

6. Open pita breads. Fill each with the meat mixture, and then lettuce, tomato, cucumber, and yogurt.

Robust Beef Barbecue Sandwiches

Makes 12-15 servings
Prep. Time: 20 minutes ❧ Cooking Time: 11-12 hours
Ideal slow-cooker size: 5-quart

3½-lb. chuck roast
¼ cup water
½ tsp. salt
½ tsp. freshly ground pepper
2 medium-sized onions, chopped
1 green bell pepper, diced
1½ cups ketchup
3 Tbsp. cider vinegar
3 Tbsp. lemon juice
2 Tbsp. Worcestershire sauce
1½ tsp. prepared mustard
3 Tbsp. brown sugar
½ tsp. chili powder
pinch cayenne pepper
Kaiser rolls *or* hamburger buns

1. Place roast in slow cooker with water. Sprinkle with salt and pepper.
2. Cook on Low for 8 hours, until beef is tender.
3. Remove lid and allow roast to cool off a bit while you mix the rest of ingredients.
4. Mix together the remaining ingredients.
5. Shred the roast using 2 forks, being careful not to scratch the inner crock or else putting the roast on a cutting board for this operation.
6. Pour sauce with onions and peppers over the shredded beef in the slow cooker. Stir. Cover, and cook on High for 3-4 hours.
7. Use a slotted spoon to serve on rolls or buns.

TIP

If the barbecue is saucier than you like it, remove the lid and cook on High until the liquid has reduced somewhat.

Why I like this recipe —
Sometimes I want to make barbecue from scratch, starting off with the basics. Of course, I do sometimes use leftover roast beef instead of cooking the roast first. And I do keep a bottle of barbecue sauce in the fridge. But it's nice to know how to create that flavor with pantry staples!

Pita Burgers

Makes 12 servings

Prep. Time: 15–20 minutes ❦ Cooking Time: 4–6 hours
Ideal slow-cooker size: 4-quart

2 lbs. lean ground chuck

1 cup dry oatmeal

1 egg

1 medium onion,
finely chopped

15-oz. can tomato sauce

2 Tbsp. brown sugar

½ tsp. salt

2 Tbsp. cider vinegar

1 Tbsp. Worcestershire sauce

1 Tbsp. soy sauce

12-slice pkg. pita bread

1. Combine the ground chuck, dry oatmeal, egg, and chopped onion in a mixing bowl. Shape the mixture into 12 burgers.

2. In a medium-sized bowl, combine the tomato sauce, brown sugar, salt, vinegar, Worcestershire sauce, and soy sauce.

3. Dip each burger in the sauce, and then stack them into your slow cooker. Pour any remaining sauce over the burgers in the cooker.

4. Cover. Cook on Low 4–6 hours, or until the burgers are as cooked as you like them.

5. Invite everyone who's eating to lift a burger out of the cooker with tongs and put it into a pita pocket with some dribbles of sauce.

Stuffed Acorn Squash

Makes 6-8 servings
Prep. Time: 45 minutes ❦ Cooking Time: 5-8 hours
Ideal slow-cooker size: 6-quart

2 acorn squash

1 lb. ground beef

1 small onion, chopped

5 cups chopped,
unpeeled apples, *divided*

4 tsp. curry powder

½ tsp. cardamom

½ tsp. ginger

scant ½ tsp.
black pepper

½ lb. sharp cheddar
cheese, cubed

6 Tbsp. apricot
preserves

1-1¼ tsp. salt

2 Tbsp. butter

scant ½ tsp. cinnamon

scant ½ tsp. nutmeg

TIP

Don't be flummoxed
by all the steps in this
recipe. You can always cook
the squash one day, and
the meat-fruit mix the
next day. Or the other
way around.

1. Wash the squash, and then cut them in half from top to bottom. Scrape out the seeds and stringy stuff. (A grapefruit spoon works well because of its teeth. But a regular spoon with some pressure behind it works, too.) Cut each half in half again.

2. Put four quarters into the bottom of the slow cooker side by side, cut side up. Set the other four quarters on top, but staggered so they're not sitting inside the four pieces on the bottom. Add about 2 Tbsp. water to the cooker. Cover. Turn the cooker to Low and let it go for 3-6 hours, or until you can stick a fork into the skin of the squash halves with very little resistance.

3. Sometime during those 3-6 hours, brown the beef and onions in a good-sized skillet. Drain off the drippings.

4. Stir 2 cups chopped apples into beef and onions. Mix in curry powder, cardamom, ginger, and black pepper.

5. Then add the cubed cheese, apricot preserves, and salt. Stir together gently. Set aside until squash is done softening up.

6. When squash is tender, divide the meat mixture among the 8 quarters evenly.

7. Put the filled quarters back into the cooker in staggered layers.

8. Cover. Cook on High for 45-60 minutes, or until the stuffing is heated through and the cheese is melted.

9. Sauté the remaining 3 cups apple slices in butter just until they're tender. Season lightly with cinnamon and nutmeg.

10. Remove the filled squash from cooker. Place a quarter on each serving plate. Top each with sautéed apples.

Seven-Layer Casserole

Makes 12-15 servings
Prep. Time: 20 minutes ❦ Cooking Time: 6-8 hours
Ideal slow-cooker size: 4-quart

1 cup uncooked rice

12-oz. can whole kernel corn, undrained

2 8-oz. cans tomato sauce, *divided*

1 cup water, *divided*

½ cup chopped onion

½ cup chopped green pepper

2 lbs. ground beef

1 tsp. salt

¼-½ tsp. pepper, whichever you like

6–8 slices lean bacon

1. Grease your slow cooker well. Spread the uncooked rice over the bottom of the cooker. Spoon the corn over top of the rice, including the juice from the corn.

2. In a bowl, mix together 1 can of tomato sauce with ½ cup water. Spoon over the corn. Sprinkle with the onion and green pepper.

3. Crumble the uncooked ground beef over the vegetables.

4. Combine the remaining can of tomato sauce with ½ cup water. Stir in the salt and pepper. Spoon over the meat.

5. Cut the bacon slices into fourths and arrange over top.

6. Cover. Cook on Low 6–8 hours, or until the vegetables and beef are as tender as you like them. Uncover the cooker during the last 15 minutes so that the bacon gets a bit crispy.

Cook's Note

Sometimes I prefer to put this Casserole into a loaf pan or baking dish and set the pan or baker into the slow cooker. I get the benefit of the cooker's slow, moist heat—plus a more attractive serving dish. If you do this, cook it for the same length of time.

Easy Curried Beef

Makes 4-6 servings
Prep. Time: 20 minutes ❧ Cooking Time: 3 hours
Ideal slow-cooker size: 3-quart

1 lb. ground beef

1 onion, chopped

3 garlic cloves, finely chopped

1 Tbsp. minced fresh ginger

2 tsp. ground coriander

2 tsp. ground cumin

1 tsp. ground turmeric

¼ tsp. ground cloves

¼ tsp. cayenne pepper, *or to taste*

¾ cup tomato sauce

2 tsp. salt

2 Tbsp. sugar

¼ cup plain yogurt at room temperature

1½ cups uncooked basmati rice

TOPPING OPTIONS:

chopped fresh onion

orange sections

sliced banana

chopped papaya *or* chopped mango

chopped peanuts

raisins

flaked coconut

more plain yogurt

1. In a skillet, brown beef, onions and garlic together. Drain off any drippings.
2. Pour beef, onions, and garlic in slow cooker.
3. Add ginger, coriander, cumin, turmeric, cloves, cayenne, tomato sauce, salt, and sugar.
4. Cook on High for 3 hours. Start cooking the basmati rice according to package directions 40 minutes before you want to eat. There should be enough time for it to sit for a bit, covered, until the curry is ready.
5. Just before serving, when slow cooker is turned off, blend yogurt into beef mixture.
6. Serve over basmati rice.
7. Send your chosen toppings in small bowls around the table after the rice and curry have been passed.

Why I like this recipe —
I was served this curry by friends who visited the Swahili coast. It's delicious! And it's ridiculously fun to choose the toppings and enjoy their contrast with the curry and rice.

Homey Dried Beef Casserole

Makes 4-6 servings
Prep. Time: 25 minutes ❧ *Cooking Time: 4-6 hours*
Ideal slow-cooker size: 3-quart

2 cups fresh *or* frozen peas, not thawed

¼ cup diced onion

★ 1¼ cups homemade mushroom white sauce

¼ lb. shredded dried beef

¼ tsp. pepper

3 cups thinly sliced potatoes

salt, to taste

⅔ cup fine bread crumbs

★ TO MAKE AN EASY MICROWAVE WHITE SAUCE, USE SOUP RECIPE ON PAGE 371

1. Stir together peas, onion, mushroom sauce, dried beef, and pepper.

2. Lay potatoes in lightly greased slow cooker. Sprinkle with salt.

3. Pour dried beef mixture over potatoes. Arrange bread crumbs over top.

4. Cover and cook on Low 4–6 hours, until potatoes are soft.

Reuben Bake

Makes 6 servings
Prep. Time: 25 minutes ❦ Cooking Time: 2½–6½ hours
Ideal slow-cooker size: 5-quart

TIP

You can make your own Thousand Island dressing. Mix together 1 cup mayonnaise and ½ cup ketchup, and add a few tablespoons of sweet pickle relish or chopped pickle.

1½ cups Thousand Island salad dressing

¾ cup sour cream *or* Greek yogurt

½ cup diced onion

12 slices dark rye *or* pumpernickel bread, cubed, *divided*

1 lb. sauerkraut, drained

1 lb. sliced corned beef, cut into bite-sized pieces

2 cups shredded Swiss cheese

2 Tbsp. butter, melted

paprika

1. In a mixing bowl, stir together dressing, sour cream or yogurt, and onion. Set aside.

2. Lightly grease slow cooker crock. Arrange bread cubes in bottom, setting aside about 1½ cups to use for the top.

3. Top the bread evenly with the sauerkraut, followed by the corned beef.

4. Spread dressing mixture over corned beef. Sprinkle with Swiss cheese.

5. Top with remaining bread cubes. Drizzle with melted butter and sprinkle with paprika.

6. Cover and cook on High for 2–3 hours or Low for 4–6 hours, until bubbly. Remove lid and continue to cook on High for 20–30 minutes until some of the moisture has evaporated.

*Why I like this recipe —
I want to have more recipes for sauerkraut than just our traditional New Year's Day pork and kraut. Once, I had some baby spinach to use up, so I added it between the sauerkraut and corned beef with excellent results. I especially love taking this Bake to potlucks, where it's always a hit.*

Beef and Wild Rice Casserole

Makes 8 servings

Prep. Time: 25 minutes ❦ Cooking Time: 6 hours

Ideal slow-cooker size: 4- or 5-quart

1 cup uncooked wild rice, rinsed and drained

1 cup chopped celery

1 cup chopped carrots

1 large onion, chopped

1 clove garlic, minced

3 beef bouillon cubes

1 tsp. garlic salt

¾ tsp. salt

2-lb. boneless round steak, cut into 1-inch cubes

3 cups water

½ lb. fresh button mushrooms, sliced

½ cup slivered almonds

1. Place all ingredients, except mushrooms and almonds, into the slow cooker, in the order listed.

2. Cover. Cook on Low 6 hours, or until the rice is tender.

3. Fifteen minutes before end of cooking time, stir in mushrooms and almonds. Cover and continue cooking.

4. Stir before serving so that everything is thoroughly mixed.

Try these changes if you want —

- *Brown beef in saucepan in 2 Tbsp. oil before putting into the slow cooker for deeper flavor.*

- *Add a bay leaf and 4–6 whole peppercorns to mixture before cooking. Remove before serving.*

- *Substitute chicken legs and thighs (skin removed) for beef.*

Why I like this recipe—
Wild rice takes a long time to cook on the stove-top. And then it takes some watching so it doesn't cook dry. I like mixing it with ingredients that also need a while to cook—and you end up with a complete meal at the end of the cooking time. This is rich and hearty.

Pastitsio

Makes 12-15 servings
Prep. Time: 35-45 minutes   *Cooking Time: 4½-5½ hours*
Ideal slow-cooker size: 5-quart

1 medium onion, chopped

1½ lbs. ground beef

1 cup tomato sauce

1 tsp. salt

¼ tsp. pepper

½ tsp. dried oregano

1 tsp. ground allspice

½ tsp. ground cinnamon

½ lb. uncooked macaroni

4 eggs, *divided*

¾ cup milk

1 cup freshly grated
Parmesan cheese, *divided*

½ cup half-and-half

2 Tbsp. flour

¼ tsp. ground nutmeg

1. Saute onion and beef together in skillet. Turn off heat. Drain excess fat.

2. Stir tomato sauce, salt, pepper, oregano, allspice, and cinnamon into meat and onions. Set aside to cool.

3. In a mixing bowl, mix uncooked macaroni, 1 egg, milk, and ¼ cup Parmesan.

4. Place macaroni mixture in greased slow cooker.

5. Whisk an egg into the cooled tomato-meat sauce. Pour it over the macaroni in the slow cooker.

6. In the mixing bowl that the macaroni came out of, place 2 remaining eggs, flour, and half-and-half. Whisk well. Add remaining ¾ cup Parmesan and whisk again.

7. Gently pour the half-and-half mixture over the tomato sauce layer, trying not to disturb it if possible. Sprinkle with nutmeg.

8. Cover and cook on Low for 4-5 hours, until macaroni is soft and sauce is bubbling around the edges.

10-Layer Slow-Cooker Supper

Makes 6-8 servings
Prep. Time: 30 minutes ❧ Cooking Time: 4-5 hours
Ideal slow-cooker size: 4-quart

1½ lbs. ground beef

6 medium potatoes, peeled or not, sliced thin (get out your mandolin)

1 medium onion, sliced thin (sharpen your paring knife)

1 cup sliced carrots

½ cup chopped green bell pepper

½ cup chopped celery

1 lb. frozen, *or* 15-oz. can, corn, drained

1 tsp. salt

¼-½ tsp. pepper, whichever you prefer

★ 10¾-oz. can cream of mushroom soup

¼ cup milk

1 lb. frozen peas

¾ cup grated sharp cheese

★ TO MAKE YOUR OWN CREAM SOUP, SEE PAGES 370-371.

TIP

Tell everyone to dig deep so they don't miss anything.

1. Brown the ground beef in a skillet. Stir often, turning it upside down and moving it around, until there's no pink left in the meat. Drain off drippings. Set the meat aside until needed.

2. Grease your slow cooker well. Then stack in layers—in this order—potatoes, onions, carrots, green peppers, celery, and corn.

3. Top with a layer of ground beef. Sprinkle with salt and pepper.

4. In a bowl, mix soup and milk together until smooth. Pour over other ingredients in cooker.

5. Cook on High 4-5 hours, or until the veggies are as tender as you like them.

6. Fifteen minutes before the end of the cooking time, add a layer of peas, followed by a layer of cheese. Cover and continue cooking 15 more minutes.

Why I like this recipe —
If you've got the right tools (mandolin, good sharp paring knife), this doesn't take long to prepare. It's fun to stack the layers, and even more fun to eat.

Mexican Haystacks

Makes 10-12 servings
Prep. Time: 20 minutes ❧ Cooking Time: 1-3 hours
Ideal slow-cooker size: 5-quart

2 lbs. ground beef

1 small onion, chopped

2 8-oz. cans tomato sauce

2 15-oz. cans chili beans with chili gravy, *or* red beans

2 10-oz. cans mild enchilada sauce, *or* mild salsa

½ tsp. chili powder

1 tsp. garlic salt

pepper to taste

cooked rice, *or* baked potatoes (made in a second slow cooker!)

CONDIMENTS, CHOOSE SOME OR ALL:

raisins

chopped apples

fresh pineapple chunks

shredded lettuce

chopped tomatoes

shredded coconut

shredded Monterey Jack cheese

corn chips

1. Brown beef in a skillet. Using a slotted spoon, lift it out of the drippings and into the slow cooker. Discard drippings.

2. Stir onion, tomato sauce, chili beans, enchilada sauce, chili powder, garlic salt, and pepper into the beef in the slow cooker.

3. Cover. Cook on Low 2-3 hours, or on High 1 hour.

4. Serve over baked potatoes or rice. Then add as many condiments on top as you want.

TIP

You can make everything in advance, including the toppings. Put them in serving bowls, cover them, and then refrigerate until the hot food is ready.

Why I like this recipe—
This is a perfect buffet meal. There's got to be at least one topping that everyone can eat. Usually, guests are surprised to see how large their haystacks are when they've finished serving themselves. I like the easy atmosphere and the way conversation unfolds when everyone is up, moving around, and filling their plates.

Main Dishes

Pasta, Grain, and Meatless

The Best Slow-Cooker Lasagna, page 141

The Best Slow-Cooker Lasagna

Makes 6-8 servings
Prep. Time: 25 minutes 🌿 Cooking Time: 4 hours
Ideal slow-cooker size: 6-quart

1 lb. ground beef

1 onion, chopped

24-oz. jar your favorite spaghetti sauce

3½ cups grated mozzarella cheese, *divided*

½ cup freshly grated Parmesan

1½ cups cottage cheese

8-oz. pkg. lasagna noodles, uncooked

1. Brown the ground beef and onion together in a large skillet until the beef is deeply browned in spots and the onion is softened. Drain off grease.

2. Stir in spaghetti sauce. Set aside.

3. In a bowl, combine 3 cups mozzarella, Parmesan, and cottage cheese. Set aside.

4. Spray the inside crock with cooking spray. Now start to build the lasagna layers in the slow cooker.

5. Place one-fourth of the meat sauce on bottom of crock.

6. Place one-third of the noodles over it, breaking them to fit if needed.

7. Spoon one-third of the cheese mixture over the noodles.

8. Repeat these layers two more times.

9. Spread the remaining one-fourth of meat sauce on the top. Sprinkle with reserved ½ cup mozzarella.

10. Cover and cook on Low for 3½-4 hours, until noodles are tender and sauce is bubbling at edges.

Why I like this recipe—
This is the easiest lasagna ever! I love the convenience of using uncooked noodles without sacrificing good texture and taste.

"Baked" Ziti

Makes 8-10 servings

Prep. Time: 15-20 minutes ❦ Cooking Time: 4 hours ❦ Standing Time: 15 minutes
Ideal slow-cooker size: 5-quart

1 lb. cottage cheese

2 Tbsp. Parmesan cheese

1 egg

1 tsp. parsley flakes

⅛ tsp. pepper

⅛ tsp. salt

1 tsp. dried minced garlic

45-oz. jar of your favorite spaghetti sauce, *divided*

14-oz. jar of your favorite spaghetti sauce, the same or different from the one above, *divided*

1 lb. ziti, uncooked

½ lb. mozzarella cheese, grated

1. Blend cottage cheese, Parmesan cheese, egg, parsley, pepper, salt, and garlic together.

2. Pour 2 cups spaghetti sauce into your greased slow cooker.

3. Drop ⅓ of the uncooked ziti over the spaghetti sauce.

4. Spoon ⅓ of the cottage cheese mixture over the ziti.

5. Repeat the layers 2 more times. You should have 1 cup spaghetti sauce left.

6. Pour the remaining tomato sauce over top.

7. Cover. Cook on Low for 4 hours.

8. Thirty minutes before the end of the cooking time, sprinkle the top of the ziti mixture with mozzarella cheese. Do not cover. Continue cooking 30 more minutes.

9. Let stand 15 minutes before serving to let everything firm up.

*Why I like this recipe —
I get a charge out of layering pasta dishes into the slow cooker and having them come out all melted together. Pick any kind of tomato sauce, with all kinds of extra ingredients in it, for this recipe. It's not finicky at all.*

Pasta Vanessa

Makes 6 servings
Prep. Time: 30 minutes ❦ *Cooking Time: 4-6 hours*
Ideal slow-cooker size: 5-quart

2 medium onions, chopped

1 yellow bell pepper, chopped

1 orange bell pepper, chopped

4 links sweet Italian sausage, chopped and skinned, about 1½ cups total

2 links hot Italian sausage, chopped and skinned, about 1 cup total

10¾-oz. can tomato purée

3 6-oz. cans tomato sauce

6-oz. can tomato paste

1 cup water

salt, to taste

pepper, to taste

1½ tsp. Italian seasoning

¼ tsp. fennel seeds

3 cloves garlic, chopped fine

2 Tbsp. honey

¾ cup heavy whipping cream

1 lb. whole wheat rotini pasta

2 Tbsp. chopped fresh parsley

1. In a large skillet, sauté onions, bell peppers, and sausage. Allow to brown in spots, stirring occasionally.

2. Carefully scrape the vegetables and sausage into the slow cooker, being sure to get all the browned bits. Add tomato purée, sauce, paste, and water. Blend well.

3. Cook on Low 4-6 hours.

4. Season with salt, pepper, Italian seasoning, fennel, and garlic. Then stir in honey.

5. Cook on Low 30-60 minutes.

6. Bring a pot of water to boil for the pasta.

7. Separately, warm the heavy whipping cream in the microwave or a small saucepan until steaming hot. Just before serving, add whipping cream to tomato mixture. Now that the two are combined, turn off the slow cooker and do not allow the sauce to boil.

8. Serve sauce over cooked rotini. Sprinkle with fresh parsley.

Why I like this recipe —
This is a happy marriage of cream and spaghetti sauce, luscious but not heavy. It really is worthy of special-occasion menus, although it doesn't take fancy ingredients.

Smokehouse Spaghetti

Makes 6 servings

Prep. Time: 30 minutes ❧ Cooking Time: 6¼-8¼ hours

Ideal slow-cooker size: 4-quart

¼ lb. bacon

1 lb. ground beef

1 medium onion, chopped

2 8-oz. cans tomato sauce

4-oz. can mushrooms with juice

1½ tsp. salt

⅛ tsp. pepper

½ tsp. oregano

½ tsp. garlic salt

8 oz. uncooked spaghetti

¼ lb. provolone cheese, grated

¼ lb. cheddar cheese, grated

1. Brown the bacon in a skillet. Drain off the drippings. Put the slices of crispy bacon on a paper-towel-lined plate to drain.

2. Brown ground beef in the skillet. Remove the beef with a slotted spoon and put it into your slow cooker. Save the drippings.

3. Cook the onion in the drippings, just until it's soft. Stir it into the slow cooker, too. Break up the bacon and add it to the cooker.

4. Stir the tomato sauce, mushrooms with their juice, and seasonings into the slow cooker.

5. Cover. Cook on Low 5½-7½ hours.

6. Stir the uncooked spaghetti into the sauce. Break it in half if that makes it easier. Cover. Cook on Low 30 minutes.

7. Uncover. Sprinkle with the two cheeses. Continue cooking for 10-15 minutes, until the cheeses have melted.

Cheese Tortellini and Meatballs with Vodka Pasta Sauce

Makes 4-6 servings
Prep. Time: 10 minutes ❧ Cooking Time: 6 hours
Ideal slow-cooker size: 5-quart

1½-lb. bag frozen cheese tortellini

1½-lb. bag frozen Italian-style meatballs

20-ounce jar vodka pasta sauce

8-oz. can tomato sauce

1 cup water

½ tsp. red pepper flakes, *or* less if you want

1½ tsp. dried oregano

1½ tsp. dried basil

2 cups grated mozzarella cheese

1. Combine all ingredients except cheese in a greased slow cooker.

2. Cook on Low for 6 hours.

3. Top each individual serving with grated cheese.

Downright Flavorful Macaroni and Cheese

Makes 6 servings
Prep. Time: 15 minutes   Cooking Time: 3-4½ hours
Ideal slow-cooker size: 4-quart

8 oz. elbow macaroni, uncooked

3 cups shredded sharp cheddar,
or Swiss cheese, *divided*

12-oz. can evaporated milk

1½ cups milk (can be skim, whole,
or somewhere in between)

2 eggs

1 tsp. salt

¼ tsp. black pepper

½ tsp. dry mustard, *optional*

2 Tbsp. minced onion, *optional*

1. Combine all ingredients, except 1 cup cheese, in greased slow cooker. Sprinkle reserved cup of cheese over top.

2. Cover. Cook on Low 3-4 hours. Do not remove the lid or stir until the mixture has finished cooking.

3. If you'd like a bit of a crusty top, cook the macs for 4 hours and 15 minutes. Uncover the cooker. Cook another 15 minutes.

Easy Mac & Cheese

QUICK and EASY

Makes 4-6 servings
Prep. Time: 10 minutes   Cooking Time: 2-3 hours
Ideal slow-cooker size: 4-quart

1 Tbsp. butter

1½ cups uncooked macaroni

3 cups milk

2-3 cups grated sharp cheese, a mixture of your favorite kinds makes the best flavor

½ tsp. salt

¼ tsp. black pepper

¼ tsp. dry mustard

1. Rub the butter in the inner crock to grease it.

2. Add rest of ingredients to cooker and mix well.

3. Cover and cook on Low for 2-3 hours, until set and macaroni is soft. Turn to High with the lid off for 20 minutes if there's water at the edges and you want it gone.

TIP
Pair it with something crisp – add a bag of baby carrots – and lunch is served!

Why I like this recipe —
It's such an easy, quick meal from pantry staples. Not only is this a favorite kid food, it's easy enough for them to help assemble and most kids love cooking! Now, to be sure, the texture of macaroni and cheese made in the slow cooker is different from a stovetop or oven-baked dish. It's a soft, uniform texture with great cheesy flavor.

Slow-Cooker Pizza

Makes 4-6 servings
Prep. Time: 40 minutes ✳ Cooking Time: 2 hours
Ideal slow-cooker size: 5- or 6-quart

1 Tbsp. olive oil

1½ cups buttermilk baking mix (like Bisquick)

⅓ cup very hot water

1½ cups pizza sauce, *divided*

your choice of pizza toppings— cooked hamburger, chipped ham *or* smoked turkey, broccoli florets, sautéed onions, sliced mushrooms, for example

1–2 cups shredded mozzarella cheese

1. Drizzle olive oil on the bottom of your slow cooker. Using a paper towel, wipe it around the sides, too.

2. Mix the baking mix and hot water together in a bowl until it forms a smooth ball.

3. Using your fingers, or a rolling pin, stretch the ball until it's about 4 inches bigger around than the bottom of your cooker. Put the ball of dough into the cooker, spreading it out so that it reaches up the sides of the cooker by an inch or so the whole way around.

4. Pour 1 cup sauce on top of the crust. Spread it out so that it covers the crust evenly.

5. Scatter pizza toppings evenly over the sauce.

6. Spoon another cup of sauce over the toppings.

7. Sprinkle evenly with cheese.

8. Cover. Cook on High for about 2 hours, or until the crust begins to brown around the edges.

9. Uncover, being careful not to let the condensation on the lid drip onto the pizza. Let stand for 15 minutes. Cut into wedges and serve.

TIP

This recipe is a very good reason to bring out the slow cooker on a weekend when everyone's hungry and nobody feels much like cooking.

Why I like this recipe —
One more thing a slow cooker can do
unexpectedly. Besides, I'm not always
in the mood to make a yeast pizza
crust. And I've had one too many bought
grocery-store crusts from a plastic bag.

Moroccan Vegetable Stew with Couscous

Makes 6 servings

Prep. Time: 30 minutes   Cooking Time: 5 hours
Ideal slow-cooker size: 6-quart

STEW:

6 cups water

¼ cup olive oil

2½ cups ½"-thick carrot chunks

2½ cups ½"-thick sweet potato slices, peeled *or* unpeeled

2½ cups ½"-thick onion wedges

2½ cups shredded green cabbage

15-oz. can garbanzo beans, rinsed and drained

1 cup chopped celery

2 cinnamon sticks

1 tsp. ground cumin

1 tsp. ground turmeric

1 tsp. salt, *or* to taste

½ tsp. ground black pepper, *or* to taste

½ cup fresh parsley leaves

COUSCOUS:

2 cups dry couscous

★ 4 cups boiling vegetable broth

¼ cup chopped fresh parsley *or* spinach

★ TO MAKE YOUR OWN BROTH, SEE PAGE 358.

1. To make the Stew, combine water, oil, carrots, sweet potatoes, onions, cabbage, beans, celery, cinnamon sticks, cumin, turmeric, salt, and pepper in a slow cooker.

2. Cook on Low for 5 hours or more, until the vegetables are as tender as you like them.

3. Stir in the fresh parsley. Add more cumin, salt, and pepper if you want.

4. Fifteen minutes before the end of the cooking time, heat the vegetable broth to a boil.

5. Place the dried couscous in a good-sized bowl. Pour the boiling broth over the couscous. Allow to sit for 5 minutes.

6. Fluff with fork. Add parsley or spinach, fluffing and stirring gently.

7. Serve the hot stew over the couscous.

Chiles Rellenos

Makes 6-8 servings
Prep. Time: 25 minutes ✂ Cooking Time: 3½-4½ hours
Ideal slow-cooker size: 6-quart

8-oz. can whole green chiles

½–1 lb. Monterey Jack cheese, cut in strips 1" wide, 3" long, ¼" thick, one stick per chile

4 large eggs

¼ cup all-purpose flour

1¼ cups milk

½ tsp. salt

black pepper to taste

⅓ cup shredded sharp cheddar cheese

paprika

TIP

Good go-alongs are beans and rice, tortillas, a crisp green salad, or pan-fried cabbage

1. Rinse seeds from chiles. Spread in single layer on paper toweling. Carefully pat dry with more toweling.

2. Split chiles open and insert stick of cheese in each one.

3. Beat eggs in a mixing bowl. Gradually add flour, beating until smooth. Add milk, salt, and pepper. Beat thoroughly.

4. Arrange stuffed chiles in shallow greased baking pan that can fit in your slow cooker. Sprinkle with cheddar cheese and paprika. Carefully pour egg mixture over all.

5. Place pan on small trivet or metal jar rings in slow cooker. Prop the slow cooker lid open at one end with a chopstick or wooden spoon handle.

6. Cook on High for 3½-4½ hours, until set and bubbling at edges.

Why I like this recipe —
This is an attractive, tasty dish for a special brunch or a potluck contribution. It never fails to turn heads.

Yummy Mexican Lasagna

Makes 6-8 servings

Prep. Time: 10-15 minutes ❧ Cooking Time: 3-4 hours
Ideal slow-cooker size: 5- or 6-quart

½ lb. ground beef

½ lb. sweet Italian sausage, squeezed out of its casings

¼ cup chopped red onion

1 tsp. garlic powder

1 tsp. cumin

¾ tsp. salt

½ tsp. pepper

14½-oz. can petite diced tomatoes

4-oz. can diced green chile peppers

1 cup chunky salsa, as hot *or* mild as you like

12 corn tortillas (6"), *divided*

15-oz. can black beans, rinsed and drained, *divided*

1 cup frozen corn kernels, *divided*

2 cups shredded cheddar cheese, *divided*

1 cup shredded Monterey Jack cheese, *divided*

2¼-oz. can sliced black olives, drained

6 small spring onions, sliced

1 large fresh tomato, chopped

1 avocado, coarsely chopped

¼ cup chopped fresh cilantro

1. Brown beef and sausage in large skillet, breaking up clumps. Drain off any drippings.

2. Stir in chopped red onion, garlic powder, cumin, salt, pepper, petite diced tomatoes, green chile peppers, and salsa.

3. Grease interior of slow cooker crock. Place ¼ of meat-vegetable mixture in bottom of crock.

4. Top with 4 corn tortillas, breaking to fit as needed.

5. Top with ⅓ of drained black beans.

6. Top with ⅓ of corn kernels.

7. Mix cheeses together in bowl. Top corn kernels with ¼ of cheese mixture.

8. Repeat all layers twice, ending with cheese.

9. Cover. Cook on Low 3-4 hours, or until heated through and cheese has melted.

10. Remove lid. Let stand 10 minutes before serving.

11. Top individual servings with a scattering of black olive slices, green onion slices, chopped fresh tomatoes, chopped avocado, and chopped fresh cilantro.

Why I like this recipe—

    This is a beautiful casserole with its fresh toppings and excellent flavors. It's nice to impress guests and yet feel calm and relaxed at mealtime because you did the easy prep a few hours ago.

Fruited Wild Rice Pilaf

Makes 4 servings
Prep. Time: 10 minutes ❦ Cooking Time: 2-3 hours
Ideal slow-cooker size: 3-quart

2 Tbsp. butter

½ cup uncooked brown rice

½ cup uncooked wild rice

1 tsp. dried savory

½ tsp. dried sage

1 small onion, chopped

⅔ cup dried cranberries

½ cup chopped dried apples

★ 2 cups chicken stock

★ TO MAKE YOUR OWN STOCK, SEE PAGE 357.

1. Use butter to grease inside of slow cooker.

2. Place rest of ingredients in slow cooker and stir gently once or twice.

3. Cover and cook on High for 2-3 hours, until rice is cooked.

TIP

Peek **through** the lid until you're pretty sure the rice is done, because lifting the lid too often will dissipate the cooking steam the rice needs.

Why I like this recipe —
This is a lovely, convenient pilaf to have next to grilled pork chops or sausage. Rice has a sweet spot in the slow cooker — it can be undercooked in the middle or turn to mush, so be willing to pay attention and get to know what works for your slow cooker the first time you cook rice.

Wild Rice Pilaf

Makes 8 servings

Prep. Time: 20 minutes   ✽   *Cooking Time: 2-3 hours*

Ideal slow-cooker size: 2- or 3-quart

¾ cup chopped onion

2 cups chopped celery

1 Tbsp. olive oil

1¼ cups wild rice, uncooked, rinsed and drained

⅓ cup pitted, chopped dates

½ tsp. dried sage

1 tsp. dried parsley

pinch black pepper

★ 14-oz. can chicken broth

1 cup water

1 Tbsp. butter

1½ cups chopped walnuts

★ TO MAKE YOUR OWN STOCK, SEE PAGE 357.

1. Saute onion and celery in olive oil until tender.
2. Place sauté in slow cooker.
3. Add rice, dates, sage, parsley, pepper, broth, and water.
4. Cover and cook on High for 2-3 hours, until rice is tender.
5. Place butter in skillet over medium heat. Add walnuts.
6. Stir and toast walnuts. Do not walk away or get distracted because the nuts burn easily! In only 2-3 minutes, they will be fragrant and tan in spots.
7. Stir the toasted walnuts into the hot pilaf or sprinkle on individual servings.

TIP

Add some grated cheese at the end and let it melt. Garnish with chopped fresh cilantro.

Salsalito Rice

Makes 6 servings

Prep. Time: 20 minutes ❧ Cooking Time: 3-4 hours

Ideal slow-cooker size: 3-quart

TIP

You may skip the fresh veggies and spices and just mix 1 cup salsa with the brown rice and water.

3 medium-sized tomatoes, chunked

2 garlic cloves

2 Tbsp. extra-virgin olive oil

1 green bell pepper, chunked

half a small onion, chunked

1 hot red pepper, *optional*

½ tsp. ground cumin

½ tsp. dried oregano

1 tsp. chili powder

1 Tbsp. brown sugar

1 tsp. salt

2 cups brown rice, uncooked

3 cups water

1. In a food processor, purée tomatoes and garlic cloves until totally smooth.

2. Add olive oil, bell pepper, onion, and optional hot pepper. Pulse several times until vegetables are chopped but not puréed.

3. Pour vegetable mixture into slow cooker.

4. Add rest of ingredients and stir well.

5. Cover and cook on High for 3-4 hours, until rice is tender and liquid is absorbed.

Green Chili Rice

Makes 6 servings
Prep. Time: 20 minutes if rice is already cooked
Cooking Time: 3-4 hours ❧ *Standing Time: 10 minutes*
Ideal slow-cooker size: 4- or 5-quart

½ lb. block Monterey Jack cheese

24 oz. (3 cups) sour cream

1 Tbsp. minced garlic, *optional*

2 4-oz. cans chopped green chilies, drained

3½ cups cooked brown *or* white rice

salt, to taste

pepper, to taste

½ cup grated cheddar cheese

Why I like this recipe— I took this to a Christmas family gathering, and I had a flock following me around asking for the recipe. It's good anytime of the year, I've learned.

1. Cut Monterey Jack cheese into strips, each about 2" long and ¾" wide. Set aside.

2. In a small bowl, combine sour cream, optional garlic, and chilies.

3. Season rice with salt and pepper.

4. Be sure to grease your slow cooker. Spread ⅓ of the rice into the cooker. Follow that with a layer of half the sour cream mixture, topped with half the cheese strips.

5. Repeat the layers, ending with a layer of rice on top.

6. Cover. Cook on Low for 3-4 hours. You want to have the center of the rice mixture steaming hot and the cheese all saucy and melted. But you don't want to have the rice drying out and crisping up around the edges of the cooker. So check things after 3 hours.

7. Remove the lid. Scatter cheddar cheese over top. Cook an additional 10 minutes, uncovered.

8. Let stand for 10 minutes before serving.

Savory Spinach Salad with Rice

Makes 6 servings

Prep. Time: 20 minutes ❧ *Cooking Time: 2½–3 hours* ❧ *Chilling Time: 8 hours*

Ideal slow-cooker size: 3-quart

1 Tbsp. butter

1 Tbsp. sesame oil

1 small onion, chopped

1 cup long-grain brown rice, uncoooked

2 Tbsp. soy sauce

1½ cups water

1 cup Italian salad dressing

1 tsp. sugar

2 generous cups chopped fresh spinach

2 ribs celery, diced

½ cup spring onions, sliced

3 slices bacon, chopped, fried, and drained

2 hardboiled eggs, chopped, *optional*

1. Saute onion in butter and sesame oil over low heat until quite browned, about 15 minutes.

2. Scrape onion and drippings into slow cooker.

3. Add rice, soy sauce, and water. Cover and cook on High for 2½–3 hours, until water is absorbed and rice is still firm.

4. Remove rice mixture to bowl. Stir in Italian dressing and sugar. Refrigerate 8 hours or overnight.

5. Just before serving, stir in spinach, celery, spring onions, bacon, and optional eggs.

Why I like this recipe —

It's a salad, sure, but it's hearty enough for a main dish with its rice and the protein from the bacon and eggs. I like the seasoned rice by itself for lunch in the spring. Delicious!

Southwestern Lasagna

Makes 9 servings

Prep. Time: 20 minutes ❦ *Cooking Time: 3-4 hours*

Ideal slow-cooker size: 4-quart oval

1 lb. lean ground beef

1 small onion, chopped

16-oz. can fat-free refried beans

half a red bell pepper, diced

1½ tsp. dried oregano

1 tsp. chili powder

1 tsp. ground cumin

½ tsp. salt

3 garlic cloves, minced

9 uncooked lasagna noodles, *divided*

1 cup shredded Mexican-blend cheese, *divided*

1 cup salsa, whatever level of heat you like

1 cup water

2 cups plain Greek yogurt

2-oz. can sliced black olives, drained

2 spring onions, sliced

½ cup chopped fresh cilantro

1. Brown beef with onion in skillet over medium heat until no longer pink and onion is softening.
2. Stir in refried beans, peppers, oregano, chili powder, cumin, salt, and garlic.
3. Place 3 noodles in bottom of lightly greased slow cooker, breaking to fit as needed.
4. Cover with half the meat/bean mixture. Sprinkle on half the cheese.
5. Repeat layers. Top with remaining 3 noodles.
6. Mix together salsa and water. Pour over top.
7. Cover and cook on Low for 3-4 hours, until noodles are tender.
8. Spread Greek yogurt over noodles. Sprinkle with olives, spring onions, and cilantro. Use a silicone knife to slice into portions, or a spoon with a thin edge to dish out.

Lentil Rice Salad Bowl

Makes 4-6 servings
Prep. Time: 20 minutes ❧ Cooking Time: 3-4 hours
Ideal slow-cooker size: 5-quart

1 cup brown lentils, rinsed

1 cup brown long-grain rice, uncooked

1 onion, chopped

★ 3½ cups water, stock, *or* combination

1 tsp. salt, *or* less if you used salted stock

¼ tsp. freshly ground pepper

1 bay leaf

½ tsp. ground cumin

SALAD TOPPING:

2 Tbsp. fresh lemon juice

½ tsp. grated lemon peel

2 Tbsp. olive oil

½ tsp. salt

2 small cucumbers, diced

2 medium-sized tomatoes, diced

3 spring onions, sliced

⅓ cup chopped fresh basil

½ cup crumbled feta cheese

★ TO MAKE YOUR OWN STOCK, SEE PAGE 358

1. Combine lentils, rice, onion, water/stock, salt, pepper, bay leaf, and cumin in slow cooker.

2. Cook on High for 3-4 hours, until lentils and rice are tender but not mushy.

3. Remove bay leaf. Keep rice mixture in slow cooker while you prepare the salad topping. The salad will wilt if it sits in its dressing too long.

4. In a medium bowl, combine lemon juice, peel, olive oil, and salt. Whisk well.

5. Place the rest of the topping ingredients in the bowl and mix gently.

6. To serve, place a scoop of the lentil rice mixture in a soup bowl. Top with a scoop of the salad. Enjoy outside with a tall iced tea!

Caribbean-Style Rice and Beans

Makes 4 servings

Prep. Time: 10 minutes ❦ Cooking Time: 2-3 hours ❦ Standing Time: 5 minutes
Ideal slow-cooker size: 4-quart

14-oz. can light coconut milk

½ **cup water**

scant ½ tsp. ground allspice

½ tsp. salt

3 fresh thyme sprigs, *or* 1 tsp. dried thyme

1 garlic clove, sliced

1 cup long-grain white rice, uncooked

15-oz. can dark red kidney beans, drained and rinsed

1. Gently stir together all ingredients in slow cooker.

2. Cover and cook on High for 2-3 hours, until rice is tender.

Spanish Baked Corn

Makes 4-6 servings

Prep. Time: 15-20 minutes ❦ *Cooking Time: 2-2½ hours*

Ideal slow-cooker size: 3-quart

6 small corn tortillas, *divided*

⅓ cup shredded smoked cheddar *or* smoked Gouda cheese, *divided*

1 cup shredded Monterey Jack cheese, *divided*

2 cups frozen corn, *divided*

½ cup chopped onion, *divided*

2 eggs, beaten

1¼ cups buttermilk

½ tsp. dry mustard

¼ tsp. dried oregano

4-oz. can diced green chili peppers, *optional*

1. Tear 3 tortillas into bite-sized pieces. Arrange in greased slow cooker.
2. Gently mix the two cheeses in a small bowl.
3. Place half the cheese mixture on top of the torn tortillas.
4. Add half the corn and half the onions. Repeat the layers, starting with the rest of the torn tortillas.
5. In a mixing bowl, stir together eggs, buttermilk, mustard, oregano, and optional chili peppers. Gently pour over tortilla mixture.
6. Cover and cook on High for 1½-2 hours. The middle should be set and the edges browned when the dish is done. If there is too much moisture around the edges, remove the lid and cook an additional 20 minutes on High.

QUICK
and
EASY

Spinach Squares

Makes 6 servings
Prep. Time: 15 minutes 🍴 Cooking Time: 2½–3 hours
Ideal slow-cooker size: 3- or 4-quart

3 eggs

1 cup milk

1 cup all-purpose flour

1 tsp. baking powder

½ lb. Monterey Jack cheese, grated

¼ lb. jalapeño Monterey Jack cheese, grated

1½ 10-oz. frozen pkgs. chopped spinach, thawed and squeezed dry, or 1 lb. fresh spinach, chopped

1. Combine eggs, milk, flour, and baking powder in a bowl and stir until a batter forms. Stir in the cheese and spinach.

2. Spread the mixture into your greased slow cooker.

3. Cook on Low for 2½–3 hours, or until a knife inserted into the center comes out clean.

4. Let it stand for 15 minutes so that the cheeses can firm up before cutting and serving the squares.

Why I like this recipe —
Spinach has such a mild flavor, I feel a little sorry that it's had to put up with such bad press for so long. If your kids haven't had spinach before, or think they don't like it (this might include their parents, for that matter!), this is a good introductory dish. I eat the leftovers cold or at room temperature, and they're just as good as when they're warm.

Garden Vegetable Bake

Makes 4-6 servings

Prep. Time: 20 minutes ❦ Cooking Time: 2½-3 hours

Ideal slow-cooker size: 4- or 5-quart

1 cup green beans,
trimmed and halved

1 zucchini, sliced

2–3 ears corn, kernels cut off

1 onion, sliced in rings

1 bell pepper, sliced in rings

2 tomatoes, sliced

salt and pepper, to taste

¾ cup grated sharp cheese

2 Tbsp. butter

1 cup cubed bread

1. In lightly greased slow cooker, layer the vegetables in the order listed, starting with green beans and ending with tomatoes, adding a sprinkle of salt and pepper every other layer.

2. Sprinkle with cheese.

3. Cover and cook on High for 2-2½ hours, until green beans are as tender as you like them.

4. In a skillet, melt butter and add cubed bread. Stir occasionally until bread cubes are toasted.

5. Sprinkle toasted bread cubes on top of Bake, pressing down lightly. Continue cooking, uncovered, until bread warms but remains crisp.

Greek Eggplant Bake

Makes 6-8 servings
Prep. Time: 15-20 minutes 🌸 Cooking Time: 2-5 hours
Ideal slow-cooker size: 4-quart

½ cup chopped onions

½ cup chopped green bell peppers

½ cup sliced mushrooms

2 tsp. olive oil

2 8-oz. cans tomato sauce

1 tsp. Worcestershire sauce

1 Tbsp. brown sugar

½ tsp. salt

1½ tsp. dried oregano

1 tsp. minced garlic

½ cup chopped fresh parsley

1 medium-sized eggplant, peeled *or* unpeeled, sliced in ⅛"-thick slices, *divided*

1½ cups grated mozzarella cheese, *divided*

¼ cup sliced black olives

1. In a large skillet or saucepan, sauté the onions, green peppers, and mushrooms in the oil.

2. Mix sauté with tomato sauce, Worcestershire sauce, brown sugar, salt, oregano, garlic, and parsley. Combine well.

3. Layer half of the sauce mixture, half of the eggplant, and half of the cheese in the slow cooker. Repeat the layers, ending with cheese. Sprinkle with black olives.

4. Cook on Low for 4-5 hours or High 2-2½ hours.

Why I like this recipe —
    This is eggplant with a few new, delicious flavors.
In the middle of summer when the eggplants come into
market, I like to load up my cooker with this dish and
set it outside on the patio to cook. I can put corn on
the cob in my other slow cooker, and there's supper!

White Bean Casserole

Makes 6-8 servings

Prep. Time: 15-20 minutes ❦ Soaking Time: 8 hours, or overnight ❦ Cooking Time: 4½-10½ hours

Ideal slow-cooker size: 4- or 5-quart

2 cups dry white beans

4 medium onions, chopped, *or* sliced thin

4 tsp. olive oil, *divided*

½ tsp. salt

¼ tsp. pepper

2 Tbsp. chopped fresh basil *or* 2 tsp. dried

2 Tbsp. chopped fresh parsley *or* 2 tsp. dried

1 Tbsp. fresh thyme, *or* 1 tsp. dried

4 slices toasted bread

2 Tbsp. butter

1. Place the dried beans in a stockpot. Cover with 8 cups of water. Cover the pot. Let the beans soak for 8 hours, or overnight.

2. Drain off the water. Put the beans into your greased slow cooker.

3. Stir in the onions, 1 tsp. oil, salt, and pepper.

4. Cover. Cook on Low 9-10 hours, or on High 4-5 hours, or until the beans are tender but still holding their shape.

5. Thirty minutes before the end of the cooking time, stir in the herbs.

6. After stirring in the herbs, blend the toast and the 3 tsp. olive oil in the food processor. Sprinkle the bread crumbs over the vegetables. Do not cover the cooker.

7. Cut the butter into chunks. Scatter over the bread crumbs. Do not cover the cooker.

8. Turn the cooker to High and cook another 20-30 minutes.

Why I like this recipe —

It's so painless to cook soaked dried beans in a slow cooker. No fears about them cooking over or sticking. I love when the beans get creamy but not mushy. That's what happens here.

Herby Fish on a Bed of Vegetables

Makes 4-5 servings
Prep. Time: 20-30 minutes ❦ Cooking Time: 4¼ to 5¼ hours
Ideal slow-cooker size: 4- or 5-quart

8-12 little new potatoes, peeled *or* not

4 Tbsp. olive oil, *divided*

salt, to taste

pepper, to taste

2-3 leeks

8-12 plum tomatoes, sliced in half, *or* 15½-oz. can diced tomatoes, undrained

¼-½ cup diced red *or* white onion

2 tsp. dried dill

2 tsp. dried basil

4 *or* 5 4-oz. to 6-oz. white fish fillets (flounder, cod, or haddock work well)

*Why I like this recipe —
This works in the slow
cooker because you let
the denser ingredients
cook as long as they
need without killing
the delicate fish.*

1. Grease the interior of the crock.
2. Wash the potatoes well. Slice them thin. (Bring out your mandolin if you have one. If you don't, get one. You'll make this dish more often.)
3. Layer the slices into the slow cooker. Drizzle each layer with oil, using about 2 Tbsp. total. Salt and pepper each layer as you go.
4. Cut the dark green tops off each leek. Split each leak from top to bottom into quarters. Hold each quarter under running water to wash out any sand and dirt.
5. Chop into ½"-wide slices. Layer into slow cooker on top of the potatoes. Salt and pepper these layers, too.
6. Scatter tomatoes over top.
7. Cover. Cook on Low 4-5 hours, or until potatoes and leeks are as soft as you like them.
8. Meanwhile, put the chopped onion in a microwave-safe bowl. Cover and cook on High 1 minute, or just until onions are softened.
9. Add the remaining 2 Tbsp. oil to onions. Stir in dill and basil, too.
10. When the veggies are as tender as you want, lay the fish fillets on top of the vegetables. Lay the thicker ends of the fillets around the outside of the crock first; that's where the heat source is. Put the thinner fillets in the middle.
11. Spread the red onion-herb mixture over the tops of the fish.

12. Cover. Turn cooker to High and cook for 15 minutes. Using a fork, test the thicker parts of the fillets to see if they're flaky. If not, cook 5 minutes more and test again.

13. When the fish is flaky, use a fish spatula to lift the fish onto a plate. Tent with foil to keep warm.

14. Using a slotted spoon, lift out the layers of vegetables and put them on a platter or serving dish with low sides. Lay the fish over top and serve.

Soups, Stews, and Chilis

Southwestern Chili, page 207

Creamy Carrot Soup with Watercress

Makes 4-6 servings

Prep. Time: 20 minutes ❧ Cooking Time: 4½-5½ hours

Ideal slow-cooker size: 4-quart

1 lb. carrots, chopped

2 medium onions, diced

2 garlic cloves, chopped

★ 4 cups chicken stock

½ tsp. ground sage

1 tsp. sugar

pinch of cayenne pepper

salt to taste, depending on how salty your stock is

few grinds of freshly ground pepper

⅓ cup all-purpose flour

juice of one orange

1 cup heavy cream, at room temperature

1 cup chopped watercress

★ TO MAKE YOUR OWN STOCK, SEE PAGE 357.

1. Combine carrots, onions, garlic, and chicken stock in slow cooker.

2. Cover and cook on Low for 4-5 hours until carrots are tender.

3. Add sage, sugar, cayenne, salt, and pepper.

4. Use an immersion blender to purée to a smooth soup, or carefully transfer hot soup to blender and purée with lid slightly ajar. Return soup to cooker.

5. Whisk flour with orange juice in a small bowl.

6. Stir flour slurry into soup. Cover and cook on High for 30 minutes.

7. Stir in cream, stirring well. Do not allow soup to boil. Remove soup from further heat by lifting inner crock out of electrical unit if needed.

8. Serve in bowls garnished with watercress.

Why I like this recipe — This is an exquisite soup. It's elegant at a luncheon, but nice for a quiet supper at home, too.

TIP
Serve with toasted, buttered sourdough bread.

Black Bean and Ham Soup

Makes 8 servings

Prep. Time: 15-20 minutes ❦ *Cooking Time: 5-11 hours* ❦ *Standing Time: 30 minutes*

Ideal slow-cooker size: 5- or 6-quart

2 cups dry black beans

4–6 cups water

2 small onions, chopped

3 cloves garlic, minced

2 tsp. paprika

1½ tsp. cumin

¼ tsp. chili powder

2 bay leaves

1 ham hock

1 green bell pepper, chopped

1. Pour the beans into a large soup pot. Cover with water. Soak or pre-cook them (covered) for 30 minutes. Pour off the water.

2. Pour the beans into your slow cooker. Add 4–6 cups fresh water to the beans.

3. Add the onions, garlic, paprika, cumin, chili powder, and bay leaves. Stir together well.

4. Submerge the ham hock in the liquid as well as you can.

5. Cover. Cook on Low for 9–11 hours, or on High for 5–7 hours, or until beans and meat are tender.

6. Thirty minutes before the end of the cooking time, stir in the chopped green pepper.

7. When the Soup is finished cooking, lift out the ham hock with a slotted spoon. Allow to cool enough to handle. Pull or cut the meat off the bone, cut into small pieces, and stir back into the soup.

8. Serve the Soup as is, or over cooked rice.

Creamy Potato Soup

Makes 6-8 servings
Prep. Time: 20 minutes ❦ Cooking Time: 6-6½ hours
Ideal slow-cooker size: 4-quart

6 potatoes, peeled and quartered

2 ribs celery, chunked

½ cup sweet, white onion, coarsely chopped

2 garlic cloves, peeled

2 cups water

1 chicken bouillon cube

2½ cups whole milk

1 Tbsp. flour

1 cup grated sharp cheese

½ tsp. dried thyme

¼ tsp. freshly ground pepper

½ tsp. salt, *or to taste*

pats of butter, *optional*

1. In slow cooker, place potatoes, celery, onion, garlic, water, and chicken bouillon cube.

2. Cover and cook on Low for 5½-6 hours until vegetables are tender.

3. Use a potato masher to mash well right in the slow cooker, keeping the slow cooker on Low.

4. In a small pan or microwave-safe bowl, whisk the flour into the milk until smooth. Warm the milk in the microwave or a small pan on the stove until warm to the touch but not hot.

5. Pour the warm milk slowly into the hot mash in the slow cooker, stirring.

6. Add cheese, thyme, pepper, and salt. Stir again and taste for salt.

7. Cover and cook on Low an additional 30 minutes, but do not allow to boil.

8. If you wish, place a butter pat in each soup bowl before ladling soup on top. The butter melts, floats to the top, and looks great!

Why I like this recipe —
I got this recipe from friends who are quite busy, but still manage to invite friends over once a week for a simple meal. Using the slow cooker allows them to come home just before their guests with the house smelling good and the meal mostly ready.

Vegetarian African Peanut Soup

Makes 4-6 servings
Prep. Time: 20 minutes ❧ Cooking Time: 7-8 hours
Ideal slow-cooker size: 5-quart

2 Tbsp. butter

1 yellow onion, diced

1 red bell pepper, diced

1 small sweet potato, peeled *or* not, diced

14½-oz can diced tomatoes with juice

½ cup uncooked pearl barley

★ 4 cups vegetable broth

3 cups water

1 Tbsp. soy sauce

1" piece ginger root

½ tsp. chili powder

1 tsp. curry powder

⅛ tsp. black pepper

⅛ tsp. cayenne, *or* more to taste

⅔ cup peanut butter

1 cup chopped fresh spinach

2 cloves garlic, minced

★ TO MAKE YOUR OWN STOCK, SEE PAGE 358.

1. Melt butter in skillet. Saute onion and pepper in butter until softened.

2. Scrape onion mixture into slow cooker, being sure to get all the butter.

3. Add sweet potato, tomatoes, barley, broth, water, soy sauce, ginger root, chili powder, curry powder, pepper, and cayenne.

4. Cover and cook on Low for 7–8 hours, until barley and sweet potatoes are quite tender.

5. Add peanut butter and whisk until smooth. Add spinach and garlic. Cover and cook an additional 15–20 minutes.

Why I like this recipe —
The unique flavor of peanut butter with spices and vegetables gets me every time. I love it. This is a fun soup to start off a curry meal, but it's also just fine on its own with some flatbread and a fresh fruit salad.

East African Beef Stew

Makes 6-8 servings

Prep. Time: 20 minutes ❦ Cooking Time: 6-8 hours
Ideal slow-cooker size: 4-quart

1 lb. beef cubes

1¼ tsp. salt

¼ tsp. pepper

1 onion, chopped

1 green bell pepper, chopped

2 cups water

2 large potatoes, peeled or not, diced

1 cup diced winter squash, *or* sweet potato

2 carrots, sliced

2 garlic cloves, sliced

2 cups chopped tomatoes

1 tsp. ground cardamom

1½ tsp. chili powder, *divided*

½ tsp. paprika

1½ tsp. curry powder, *divided*

1 Tbsp. water

1 Tbsp. apple cider vinegar

1 Tbsp. cornstarch

1. Brown beef, salt, and pepper in skillet. Add and sauté onion and pepper.

2. Place beef, onions, and peppers in slow cooker, being sure to get all drippings.

3. Add water, potatoes, squash, carrots, garlic, tomatoes, cardamom, 1 tsp. chili powder, paprika, and 1 tsp. curry.

4. Cover and cook on Low for 6-8 hours, until beef and vegetables are tender.

5. Separately, whisk together water, vinegar, cornstarch, remaining ½ tsp. chili powder, and remaining ½ tsp. curry powder. Stir through the hot stew.

6. Cook an additional 15-20 minutes until thickened.

TIP

If you can acquire injera, the Ethiopian flatbread, serve the stew with it. Encourage diners to pinch up bites of the stew with a bit of injera for an authentic meal. However, you can also serve the stew with pita bread or over rice.

Why I like this recipe—
Beef stews are an essential part of winter, I think, but this one has a delightful mix of spices for the times I want a little something exotic. It's still a comforting stew, and I usually serve it with whatever bread I have on hand.

Hearty Beef Barley Soup

Makes 8 servings

Prep. Time: 15 minutes ❦ *Cooking Time: 9 hours*
Ideal slow-cooker size: 5-quart

2-lb. beef chuck roast

3 cups tomato juice

1 cup red wine

4 cups water

3 Tbsp. soy sauce

1 bay leaf

½–1 tsp. salt, to taste

¼ tsp. freshly ground pepper

1 onion, diced

2 ribs celery, finely chopped

2 carrots, diced *or* shredded

1 cup uncooked quick-cooking barley

¼ tsp. dried thyme

1. Place roast, tomato juice, wine, water, soy sauce, bay leaf, ½ tsp. salt, pepper, onion, celery, and carrots in slow cooker.

2. Cook on Low for 8 hours.

3. Remove roast. Shred or chop the meat and return it to the slow cooker.

4. Add barley and thyme. Cook 30–60 minutes more until barley is tender.

Borscht

Makes 6-8 servings
Prep. Time: 15 minutes ❧ Cooking Time: 6-8 hours
Ideal slow-cooker size: 6-quart

★ 5-6 cups beef stock, preferably homemade

1 onion, diced very fine

2 cups finely shredded green cabbage

2 medium potatoes, peeled or not, grated

1 medium beet, grated

1 carrot, grated

1 rib celery, diced very fine

2 Tbsp. tomato paste

1 Tbsp. apple cider vinegar

1 bay leaf

1 dried red pepper, *or* ⅛ tsp. cayenne

½ tsp. freshly ground black pepper

3 tsp. dried dillweed, *divided*

½ cup chopped fresh parsley

⅓-½ cup Greek yogurt, *divided*

★ TO MAKE YOUR OWN STOCK, SEE PAGE 357.

1. In slow cooker, combine 5 cups stock, onion, cabbage, potatoes, beet, carrot, celery, tomato paste, vinegar, bay leaf, red pepper, black pepper, and 2 tsp. dillweed.

2. Cover and cook on Low for 6-8 hours, until vegetables are tender.

3. Add remaining 1 tsp. dillweed and parsley. Add the other cup of stock, depending on how thick you like your soup. Taste to check salt, depending how salty your beef stock is.

4. Serve hot in bowls with a tablespoon or two of Greek yogurt dolloped on top.

TIP
Include some cooked, shredded beef. If you have beets with their tops, use the tops instead of some of the cabbage.

Why I like this recipe —
Borscht is delicious, but it really is a home recipe that varies according to ethnicity and tradition. Some people even eat borscht chilled! This is my version and I add and subtract ingredients up and down the list, depending on what I have on hand. I have added flat beer, mushrooms, and leftover diced lamb at various times, and it was all good.

Lentil Soup, Greek-Style

Makes 6-8 servings
Prep. Time: 20 minutes ❧ Cooking Time: 5-6 hours
Ideal slow-cooker size: 5-quart

2 cups dry lentils

★ 3 cups vegetable broth

3 cups water

1 onion, chopped

2 carrots, chopped

1 rib celery, chopped

1 tsp. dried oregano, *divided*

2 cloves garlic, minced

2-oz. can sliced black olives, drained

1 cup finely chopped fresh spinach

½ cup tomato sauce

several grinds of black pepper

salt, to taste

3 Tbsp. red wine vinegar

★ TO MAKE YOUR OWN STOCK, SEE PAGE 358.

1. Place lentils, vegetable broth, water, onion, carrots, celery, and ½ tsp. oregano in slow cooker.

2. Cover and cook on Low for 4-5 hours, until lentils are tender.

3. Add rest of ingredients, including remaining ½ tsp. oregano, and cook for another hour on Low.

Why I like this recipe —
It's a nice take on lentils, still using mostly pantry staples. I'm willing to keep black olives on hand for this soup!

Country Lentil Soup with Sausage

Makes 8-10 servings

Prep. Time: 25 minutes   Cooking Time: 6¼–8¼ hours
Ideal slow-cooker size: 6-quart

¼ lb. hot Italian sausage, chopped, or squeezed out of casings

¾ lb. sweet Italian sausage, chopped, or squeezed out of casings

2 cups chopped onion

1 cup chopped celery

4 carrots, sliced

2 cups dry lentils

2 cups canned tomatoes, quartered and undrained

8 cups water

1 bay leaf

1-2 tsp. salt, depending on your taste preference

¼ tsp. pepper

1 Tbsp. cider vinegar

1. Brown sausage in skillet, breaking it up and allowing it to get brown in spots. Place browned sausage in slow cooker.

2. Sauté onion and celery in remaining sausage drippings until soft. Place celery and onion in slow cooker and discard any remaining drippings.

3. Add carrots, lentils, tomatoes, water, bay leaf, salt, and pepper to slow cooker.

4. Cover and cook on Low for 6–8 hours until vegetables and lentils are soft. Break up the tomatoes further with a spoon if you wish.

5. Stir in vinegar. Cover and cook on Low for 15–20 more minutes.

Why I like this recipe —
   This is richly wonderful. After a few
bites, you'll be sure that all is well in the
world, it's that close to living a fantasy.

Creamy Tomato Basil Soup

Makes 10 servings
Prep. Time: 15 minutes ✿ Cooking Time: 4½ hours
Ideal slow-cooker size: 5- or 6-quart

½ cup diced onion

2 Tbsp. butter

1 Tbsp. minced garlic

★ 2 cups chicken stock

2 28-oz. cans crushed tomatoes

2 cups heavy cream

¼ cup chopped fresh basil, plus more for garnish

1 tsp. salt

1 tsp. white pepper

★ TO MAKE YOUR OWN STOCK, SEE PAGE 357.

1. Sauté the onions in butter in a skillet until they're transparent. Stir in the garlic and sauté for 1 more minute.

2. Put the softened onions and garlic into the slow cooker. Stir in the chicken stock and crushed tomatoes. Cover. Cook on Low 4 hours.

3. Stir in the cream, ¼ cup fresh basil, salt, and pepper. Cover. Cook on Low 30–60 minutes, or until the soup is hot through and through, but not boiling. If the soup is thicker than you like, thin it with half-and-half or milk.

4. Top the individual servings with more chopped fresh basil if you want.

Split Pea Soup with Ham

Makes 6-8 servings
Prep. Time: 15 minutes ❦ *Cooking Time: 8-14 hours*
Ideal slow-cooker size: 6-quart

1 smoked ham hock

1 onion, chopped

1 tsp. apple cider vinegar

7 cups water

3 cups dried green split peas

3 carrots, chopped

2 ribs celery, chopped

2 bay leaves

⅛ tsp. pepper

1 tsp. Worcestershire sauce

1. Place ham hock, onions, vinegar, and water in slow cooker.

2. Cover and cook on Low for 4–8 hours, however much time you have. You are essentially making a stock for your soup.

3. Add the rest of the ingredients. Continue to cook on Low for 4–6 hours, until the meat is tender, and the split peas are as soft and disintegrated as you like. We cook ours until they have fallen apart into a purée!

4. Use a slotted spoon to lift out the ham hock. Let cool until you can handle it. Take the meat off the bone, cut it up, and stir it back into the soup.

5. Check for salt and fish out the bay leaves before serving.

TIP

This soup freezes well, so make the full amount even if you're a small household, and enjoy the convenience of meals in the freezer.

Why I like this recipe —
This is plain, simple eating
that we enjoy every time.
You can add some chopped
spinach or a chopped potato,
if you wish, to Step 3.

Corn and Shrimp Chowder

Makes 6 servings
Prep. Time: 20 minutes ❦ Cooking Time: 3-4 hours
Ideal slow-cooker size: 3½-quart

4 slices bacon, diced

1 cup chopped onions

★ 2 cups diced, unpeeled red potatoes, *or* frozen hash browns

2 10-oz. pkgs. frozen corn

1 tsp. Worcestershire sauce

½ tsp. paprika

½ tsp. salt

⅛ tsp. pepper

2 cups water

2 6-oz. cans shrimp, *or* ¾ lb. cooked and peeled small shrimp

12-oz. can evaporated milk

chopped chives

★ TO MAKE YOUR OWN HASH BROWNS, SEE TIP ON PAGE 228.

1. Fry bacon in skillet until crisp. Remove and drain bacon, but keep the drippings. Add onions to drippings and sauté just until they soften.
2. Using a slotted spoon, transfer onions to slow cooker.
3. Add potatoes, corn, Worcestershire sauce, paprika, salt, pepper, and water to cooker.
4. Cover. Cook on Low 2½–3½ hours.
5. Stir in shrimp and evaporated milk. Cover. Cook 30 more minutes on Low.
6. Just before serving, stir in chives.

Curried Chicken Chowder

Makes 6-8 servings
Prep. Time: 20 minutes ❦ *Cooking Time: 6½–8½ hours*
Ideal slow-cooker size: 4- or 5-quart

2 chicken legs, bone-in, with thighs attached

5 cups water

1 onion, chopped

1 cup chopped celery, leaves included

1 medium potato, diced

3 carrots, sliced

1 cup frozen green beans

1 bay leaf

1 Tbsp. curry powder, *divided*

1½–2 tsp. salt, depending on taste preference

1 apple, peeled and diced fine

3 Tbsp. all-purpose flour

⅓ cup half-and-half, room temperature

1. Remove skin from chicken.
2. Place chicken in slow cooker with water, onion, celery, potatoes, carrots, green beans, bay leaf, half the curry powder, and salt.
3. Cover and cook on Low for 6-8 hours.
4. Remove chicken. Add apple and the rest of the curry powder. Keep slow cooker on Low.
5. Pick the meat off the bones and return meat to slow cooker.
6. In a small bowl, whisk together flour and half-and-half until completely smooth.
7. Whisk into hot soup. Cook an additional 25–30 minutes on Low, stirring once or twice, until thick and apple is softened. Fish out the bay leaf before serving.

Country Corn Chowder

Makes 5-6 servings
Prep. Time: 15-20 minutes 🍴 Cooking Time: 4¼-5¼ hours
Ideal slow-cooker size: 4- or 5-quart

4 potatoes, peeled or not, diced

1 onion, diced

1 rib celery, diced

15-oz. can cream-style corn

15-oz. can whole-kernel corn, undrained

1 cup chopped, cooked ham

15-oz. can lima beans, undrained

1 green, *or* red, bell pepper, diced

2 Tbsp. cornstarch

1¾ cups milk

salt, to taste

pepper, to taste

1. Put potatoes, onion, celery, and both kinds of corn into your slow cooker. Add about 2 inches of water.

2. Cover. Cook on Low 4–5 hours, or until potatoes are as tender as you like them.

3. Thirty minutes before the end of the cooking time, stir in the ham, lima beans, and diced bell pepper.

4. Take ½ cup of the cooking liquid from the cooker and put it into a small bowl. Stir in the cornstarch until the mixture is smooth. Pour it back into the hot soup. Stir until the liquid thickens.

5. Pour in the milk. Cover and continue cooking until the Chowder is heated through.

6. Taste. Add salt and pepper if you want. Then serve!

East Coast Chowder

Makes 6 servings

Prep. Time: 15 minutes   Cooking Time: 4½ hours
Ideal slow-cooker size: 4-quart

1 onion, chopped

2 Tbsp. butter

1 carrot, grated

1½ cups corn

4 potatoes, cubed, peeled if desired

1 tsp. salt

1 tsp. Old Bay seasoning

1 Tbsp. dried parsley

3 cups water

1 lb. frozen cod, *or* other mild white fish, thawed, cut in cubes

12-oz. can evaporated milk

1. In skillet, sauté onion in butter until soft but not brown.

2. Place sauté in slow cooker.

3. Add carrot, corn, potatoes, salt, Old Bay, parsley, and water.

4. Cover and cook on Low for 4 hours, or until potatoes are tender.

5. Add cod. Cover and cook an additional 20 minutes on Low. The cod should be cooked through in flaky, white chunks.

6. Stir in evaporated milk. Serve.

QUICK
and
EASY

Mexican Chicken Tortilla Soup

Makes 6-8 servings

Prep. Time: 15 minutes ⚭ Cooking Time: 6-8 hours

Ideal slow-cooker size: 6-quart

6 bone-in chicken thighs, skin removed

2 15-oz. cans black beans, undrained

2 15-oz. cans Mexican stewed tomatoes, *or* Rotel tomatoes

1 cup salsa—mild, medium, *or* hot, whichever you prefer

4-oz. can chopped green chilies

14½-oz. can tomato sauce

tortilla chips

2 cups grated cheese, your choice

1. Combine all ingredients except chips and cheese in large slow cooker.

2. Cover. Cook on Low 6-8 hours, or just until the meat is tender.

3. Right before serving, remove chicken thighs from the soup. Remove bones, and then cut meat into bite-sized pieces. Stir back into soup.

4. To serve, put a handful of chips in each individual soup bowl. Ladle soup over chips.

5. Top with cheese.

Brevard Stew

Makes 10 servings
Prep. Time: 30 minutes ❧ Cooking Time: 8-9 hours
Ideal slow-cooker size: 5-quart

1½ lbs. boneless chuck roast, cut in 1½" cubes

1 Tbsp. oil

1 cup onions, chopped

3 medium-sized potatoes, cut in ½" cubes

28-oz. can low-sodium crushed tomatoes, undrained

1 Tbsp. Worcestershire sauce

½ tsp. salt

16-oz. can cream-style corn, undrained

16-oz. can low-sodium lima beans, drained and rinsed

16-oz. can low-sodium cut carrots, drained and rinsed

½ tsp. dried marjoram

4 slices bacon, cooked and crumbled

¼ tsp. red pepper sauce

TIP
Add some more pepper sauce if you're looking for a little more heat.

1. In a large skillet, brown beef in olive oil over medium heat until beef is brown on all sides. Lift beef out of skillet with a slotted spoon and put the cubes into the greased slow cooker. Keep the drippings in the skillet.

2. Add the chopped onions to the skillet. Stir up the brown bits and let the onions soften for a few minutes. Add them and the pan drippings to the cooker.

3. Add the potatoes, tomatoes, Worcestershire sauce, and salt to the cooker. Mix well.

4. Cover. Cook on Low 8-9 hours.

5. Thirty minutes before serving, stir in the corn, lima beans, carrots, and marjoram. Cover and keep on cooking for half an hour.

6. Stir the bacon and red pepper sauce into the stew just before serving.

Why I like this recipe —
This is sort of a glorified vegetable soup, but without a lot of stock. Don't wolf it. Take your time tasting all the flavors and textures.

15-Bean Soup

Makes 12 servings
Prep. Time: 15 minutes ❦ Cooking Time: 10¼ hours
Ideal slow-cooker size: 6-quart

20-oz. pkg. dried **15-bean soup mix**, *or*
2¼ cups dried beans of your choice

★ 5 14½-oz. cans, *or* 9 cups,
chicken *or* vegetable broth

2 cups chopped carrots

1½ cups chopped celery

1 cup chopped onions

2 Tbsp. tomato paste

1 tsp. dried basil

½ tsp. dried oregano

¼ tsp. pepper

14½-oz. can diced tomatoes

handful fresh parsley, chopped, *optional*

★ TO MAKE YOUR OWN STOCK, SEE PAGES 357-358.

1. Combine all ingredients except tomatoes and parsley in slow cooker.
2. Cover. Cook on Low 10 hours, or until beans are tender.
3. Stir in tomatoes and optional parsley.
4. Cover. Cook on High 10–20 minutes, or until soup is heated through.

Minestrone

Makes 4-5 servings
Prep. Time: 30 minutes ❦ Cooking Time: 4½-6½ hours
Ideal slow-cooker size: 5-quart

¾ lb. sweet, *or* hot, Italian sausage

1 Tbsp. cooking oil

1 cup sliced carrots

1 cup chopped onions

½ cup sliced celery

★ 10¾-oz. can beef broth

10¾-oz. can Italian tomato soup

1½ cups water

2 small zucchini, sliced

1 cup uncooked, bow-shaped pasta

16-oz. can Great Northern beans, rinsed and drained

¼ cup chopped fresh parsley

★ TO MAKE YOUR OWN STOCK, SEE PAGE 357.

1. Dice sausage into small pieces and brown lightly in oil in skillet. Using a slotted spoon, move sausage into your slow cooker. Get rid of the drippings.
2. Stir the carrots, onions, and celery into the slow cooker. Then add the beef broth, tomato soup, and water.
3. Cover. Cook 4-6 hours on Low, or until the vegetables are as tender as you like them.
4. Add the zucchini, pasta, and drained beans.
5. Cover. Turn your cooker to High and cook 30 minutes, or more, but just until the pasta is cooked and the zucchini is softened.
6. Top individual soup bowls with parsley.

Wild Rice Soup

Makes 8-10 servings
Prep. Time: 30 minutes ❦ Cooking Time: 4½-5½ hours
Ideal slow-cooker size: 4-quart

1½ cups uncooked wild rice

2 tsp. salt, *divided*

2 Tbsp. butter, melted

2 Tbsp. minced onion

⅔ cup flour

3½ cups water

★ 4 14½-oz. cans (7 cups) chicken broth

1 tsp. salt

⅔ cup cooked minced ham

⅔ cup finely grated carrots

¼ cup slivered almonds

2 cups half-and-half (low-fat works well, too)

★ TO MAKE YOUR OWN STOCK, SEE PAGE 357.

1. Combine the rice, 2 tsp. salt, butter, onion, and flour in your slow cooker.

2. When well mixed, stir in the water and chicken broth.

3. Cover. Cook on Low 4-5 hours, or until the rice is tender.

4. Add the ham, carrots, and almonds. Cover. Continue cooking for 30 more minutes.

5. Immediately before serving, blend in the half-and-half. Let stand in the cooker so the Soup warms up, but don't let it boil after adding the half-and-half. Taste the soup to see if it needs more salt.

Why I like this recipe —
   Wild rice loves the slow moist heat of a slow cooker. Usually I'm too impatient to make it on the stove top, it takes so long. Here it's at home, and I know I've got succulent soup on the other end of the half-day of cooking.

Super Garbanzo Soup

Makes 6 servings

Prep. Time: 20 minutes ❦ Standing Time: 8 hours or overnight ❦ Cooking Time: 6 hours

Ideal slow-cooker size: 4-quart

1 lb. dry garbanzo beans

16 raw baby carrots, cut in halves, about 8 oz. total

1 large onion, diced

4 ribs celery, cut in ½"-thick slices

1 large green pepper, diced

½ tsp. dried basil

½ tsp. dried oregano

½ tsp. dried rosemary

½ tsp. dried thyme

★ 2 28-oz. cans (7 cups) vegetable broth

1 empty broth can (3½ cups) filled with water

8-oz. can tomato sauce

8 oz. prepared hummus

½ tsp. salt

★ TO MAKE YOUR OWN STOCK, SEE PAGE 358.

1. Put dried beans in slow cooker. Cover with cold water. Let soak overnight, or for 8 hours.

2. Drain off water. Return drained, soaked beans to slow cooker.

3. Add carrots, onion, celery, and green pepper.

4. Stir in basil, oregano, rosemary, and thyme.

5. Pour in broth and water.

6. Cover. Cook on High 6 hours.

7. Half an hour before the end of the cooking time, stir in tomato sauce, hummus, and salt.

8. Cover and continue cooking 30 minutes, or until the soup is hot.

TIP

Make it a party and serve with Irish soda bread and lemon curd. Or any favorite bread will do.

Pasta e Fagioli

Makes 8-10 servings
Prep. Time: 20 minutes ❦ Cooking Time: 4-6 hours
Ideal slow-cooker size: 5- or 6-quart

⅓ cup diced bacon *or* pancetta

1 cup diced onion

1 cup julienned carrot

1 cup chopped celery

★ 1 cup beef stock, and maybe a bit more

12-oz. can V-8 juice

2 14½-oz. cans diced tomatoes, undrained

15-oz. can tomato sauce

15-oz. can red kidney beans, rinsed and drained

15-oz. can Great Northern beans, rinsed and drained

2 cloves garlic, minced

1 Tbsp. vinegar

1 tsp. salt

½ tsp. freshly ground pepper

1 tsp. dried oregano

1 tsp. dried basil

½ tsp. dried thyme

½ lb. ditali pasta, tubetini, macaroni *or* other small pasta

★ TO MAKE YOUR OWN STOCK, SEE PAGE 357.

1. In a skillet, sauté the bacon or pancetta, onion, carrot, and celery for a few minutes, until bacon is curling and browned in spots and vegetables are softened. Pour into slow cooker.

2. Pour the beef stock into skillet to deglaze it and get all the good drippings and bits. Use a silicone scraper to get everything into the slow cooker.

3. Add remaining ingredients, except pasta, and stir well. Cook on Low for 4-6 hours.

4. Cook the pasta separately according to package directions. Add it to the soup. Taste the soup to check the salt and herb level. You may want to add a bit more beef stock if the soup is thicker than you like.

Why I like this recipe —
It's Italian comfort food, often made at home only for the family. You'll find this soup hearty and satisfying.

TIP
This recipe is wonderful on its own, or with crusty bread and cheese and a piece of fruit afterwards.

Black Bean, Tomato, and Corn Chili

Makes 6-8 servings
Prep. Time: 10 minutes   Cooking Time: 4-6 hours
Ideal slow-cooker size: 4-quart

2 15-oz. cans black beans, drained and rinsed

14½-oz. can Mexican stewed tomatoes, undrained

14½-oz. can diced tomatoes, undrained

11-oz. can whole-kernel corn, drained

4 spring onions, sliced

1 small green bell pepper, chopped

2–3 Tbsp. chili powder

½ tsp. ground cumin

½ tsp. salt

2 cloves garlic, minced

15-oz. jar queso, for garnish

2 spring onions, sliced, for garnish

1. Combine all ingredients except the garlic and garnishes in your slow cooker.

2. Cover. Cook on Low 4–6 hours.

3. Fifteen minutes before the end of the cooking time, stir in the garlic. Cover and continue cooking.

4. Garnish each bowl of chili with a dollop of queso and a sprinkle of spring onions.

Southwestern Chili

Makes 4 servings

Prep. Time: 10-15 minutes ❧ *Cooking Time: 4-6 hours*
Ideal slow-cooker size: 4-quart

1 Tbsp. butter

1 medium onion, chopped

2 medium raw sweet
potatoes, peeled and diced

2 15-oz. cans black beans,
rinsed and drained

2 garlic cloves, minced

1 Tbsp. chili powder

pinch cinnamon

16-oz. jar salsa, as spicy as you like

1 cup water

sour cream *or* Greek
yogurt, for garnish

fresh cilantro, chopped,
for garnish

1. Combine all ingredients in slow cooker except the sour cream and cilantro.
2. Cover and cook on Low for 4-6 hours.
3. Garnish individual bowls with sour cream or Greek yogurt and cilantro.

Why I like this recipe —
Sweet potatoes are a
delicious counterpart to
spice and heat. Amp up
the heat if that's your
thing — I only get up to
medium salsa myself —
because you can always
cool things down with a
bigger dollop of yogurt.

Chili

Makes 6 servings

Prep. Time: 30 minutes   *Cooking Time: 5-6 hours*

Ideal slow-cooker size: 5-quart

1 lb. ground round beef

3 large onions, diced

2 large green bell peppers, diced

1½ (15½-oz. size) cans stewed tomatoes, undrained

2 16-oz. cans red kidney beans, rinsed and drained

6-oz. can tomato paste

1 cup water

2 garlic cloves, chopped fine

2 Tbsp. chili powder

½ tsp. ground cumin

⅛ tsp. cayenne pepper

2 whole cloves

1 bay leaf

¼ cup plum preserves, or grape jelly

1 tsp. white vinegar

2 Tbsp. sugar

salt and pepper, to taste

1. Saute beef, onions, and peppers together in skillet until beef is browned but not entirely cooked.

2. Scrape into slow cooker. Add rest of ingredients.

3. Cover and cook on Low for 5-6 hours.

Why I like this recipe — The flavors in this chili are so good, yet not startling. It's still comfort food!

Chickpea Chili

Makes 6–8 servings

Prep. Time: 15 minutes 🍴 Cooking Time: 6–8 hours

Ideal slow-cooker size: 3-quart

1 small onion, minced

2 cloves garlic, minced

15-oz. can garbanzo beans, drained

2 8-oz. cans tomato sauce

1 Tbsp. chili powder

1 tsp. ground cumin

½ tsp. dried oregano

cayenne pepper, to taste

★ ⅔ cup low-fat plain yogurt

2 cups hot, cooked brown rice

★ TO MAKE YOUR OWN YOGURT, SEE PAGE 368.

1. Mix everything into your slow cooker except the yogurt and brown rice.

2. Cover. Cook on Low 6–8 hours.

3. To serve, place a scoop of brown rice in a soup bowl, add some Chili, and dollop yogurt over top.

Why I like this recipe — I like to bite into chickpeas. They hold their shape and character even after stewing away for hours with seasonings.

White Chili

Makes 6 servings

Prep. Time: 20-25 minutes 🌿 Cooking Time: 4-6 hours

Ideal slow-cooker size: 4-quart

1½ Tbsp. oil

1 large onion, chopped

2 cups chopped, cooked chicken

4-oz. can chopped mild green chilies

2 cloves garlic, minced

½–1 Tbsp. diced jalapeño pepper, depending on how much heat you like

1½ tsp. ground cumin

1 tsp. dried oregano

½ tsp. salt, *or more to taste*

15-oz. can Great Northern beans, rinsed and drained

★ 2½ cups chicken stock

6 oz. shredded Monterey Jack cheese

½ cup sour cream, *or* Greek yogurt, at room temperature

chopped spring onions

fresh cilantro, chopped

★ TO MAKE YOUR OWN STOCK, SEE PAGE 357.

1. In skillet, sauté onion in oil over medium heat.

2. Scrape it into slow cooker. Add chicken, chilies, garlic, jalapeño, cumin, oregano, salt, beans, and chicken stock.

3. Cook on Low for 4-6 hours.

4. Just before serving, add cheese and sour cream or yogurt. Heat just until cheese is melted, being careful not to let the soup boil.

5. Taste for seasoning, and possibly add more salt, oregano, and cumin. Serve at once, garnished with chopped spring onions and fresh cilantro in individual bowls.

Why I like this recipe —
It's a nice alternative to regular chili (which I also really like), and I love a bowlful for supper with buttered cornbread on the side.

TIP

White chili doesn't freeze well because of its dairy ingredients, but it will keep for up to a week in the fridge. Warm up a bowl every day for lunch!

Garden Vegetarian Chili

Makes 8-10 servings
Prep. Time: 20 minutes   Cooking Time: 7½-8½ hours
Ideal slow-cooker size: 5-quart

2 cups chopped carrots

1½ cups chopped green bell pepper

1 cup chopped onions

4 garlic cloves, minced

5½ cups stewed tomatoes

1 cup frozen corn

2 1-lb. cans kidney beans, undrained

1 cup raisins

¼ cup wine vinegar

2 tsp. salt

1½ tsp. cumin

¼ tsp. pepper

¼ tsp. Tabasco sauce

1 bay leaf

1½ tsp. dried oregano

¾ cup unsalted cashews

2 Tbsp. chopped parsley

1 cup grated cheese, *optional*

1. Combine all ingredients in slow cooker except oregano, cashews, parsley, and cheese.
2. Cover. Simmer on Low 7-8 hours. Add oregano and cashews. Simmer 30 minutes.
3. Garnish individual servings with parsley and optional grated cheese.

*Why I like this recipe —
This is a vegetarian chili.
That earns it a point.
And the raisins, cashews,
and dusting of cheese
earn it 3 more points.*

Turkey Pumpkin Black-Bean Chili

Makes 10-12 servings
Prep. Time: 20 minutes ✂ *Cooking Time: 7-8 hours*
Ideal slow-cooker size: 6-quart

1 cup chopped onions

1 cup chopped yellow bell pepper

3 garlic cloves, minced

1½ tsp. dried oregano

1½–2 tsp. ground cumin

2 tsp. chili powder

2 15-oz. cans black beans, rinsed and drained

2½ cups chopped cooked turkey

16-oz. can pumpkin

14½-oz. can diced tomatoes

3 cups chicken broth

1. Put all ingredients into the slow cooker. Stir till well mixed.

2. Cover. Cook on Low 7-8 hours.

TIP

If you have left-over turkey, this is a way to give it a second life in its own right.

Vegetables

Sweet Potatoes Almondine

Makes 4-6 servings
Prep. Time: 20 minutes   Cooking Time: 4–6 hours
Ideal slow-cooker size: 4-quart

4 large sweet potatoes, peeled and cut into 1" chunks

1 cup water

½ cup (1 stick) butter, melted, *divided*

⅔ cup milk

¼ tsp. salt

½ cup brown sugar

¼ tsp. pumpkin pie spice

½ cup slivered almonds

1. Put the peeled sweet potato chunks and the water into your slow cooker. Cover and cook on Low 3-5 hours, or until the potatoes are fall-apart tender.

2. Drain off the water. Mash the potatoes with a hand-held mixer or a potato masher in the slow cooker.

3. Stir in half the melted butter, the milk and salt.

4. In a separate bowl, mix together the brown sugar, pumpkin pie spice, almonds, and remaining 4 Tbsp. melted butter. Spread the topping over the mashed sweet potatoes.

5. Cover. Cook 30 minutes on Low. Take the lid off and cook another 20–30 minutes on Low, or until the potatoes are heated through and the topping has crisped up a bit.

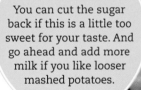

TIP
You can cut the sugar back if this is a little too sweet for your taste. And go ahead and add more milk if you like looser mashed potatoes.

Orange-Glazed Sweet Potatoes

Makes 8 servings
Prep. Time: 20-30 minutes 🍃 Cooking Time: 6-9 hours
Ideal slow-cooker size: 5-quart

8 medium sweet potatoes

½ cup water

½ tsp. salt

1 cup brown sugar, packed

2 Tbsp. cornstarch

½ tsp. shredded orange peel

2 cups orange juice

½ cup raisins

¾ stick (6 Tbsp.) butter

¼ cup chopped walnuts

TIP

Add 2 cups of dried apricot halves to the sauce, just before you pour it over the sweet potatoes.

1. Peel the sweet potatoes. Arrange them in the slow cooker. Add ½ cup water.

2. Cover. Cook on Low for 5-8 hours, or until they're tender. Discard any remaining water.

3. Take sweet potatoes out of the cooker and let them cool until you can handle them. Then cut them into slices about ½" thick.

4. While the potatoes are cooking, combine the brown sugar and cornstarch in a pan. Blend in the orange peel, the orange juice, and the raisins. Cook and stir over medium heat until thickened and bubbly. Cook 1 minute longer.

5. Add the butter and walnuts, stirring until the butter melts.

6. Put a layer of sweet potato slices into the cooker. Pour part of the sauce over top. Make a second layer. Top it with the remaining sauce.

7. Cover. Cook on High for 1 hour, or until the sweet potatoes are caramelized and glazed.

Why I like this recipe —
Fruit and sweet potatoes just work together. Make this your own recipe by adding more orange peel if you like, or more raisins, or switch from walnuts to pecans. I like that you can cook the potatoes from scratch to the glazed stage, all in your slow cooker.

Sweet Potato Pudding with Cardamom

Makes 8 servings

Prep. Time: 35 minutes ❧ Cooking Time: 4-5 hours and then 4-5 hours

Ideal slow-cooker size: 5-quart

4 lbs. sweet potatoes, about 5 large ones

1 cup water

half stick (¼ cup) butter, melted

1½ tsp. salt

a few grinds of freshly ground pepper

1 tsp. ground cardamom

2 Tbsp. brown sugar

1½ cups evaporated milk, *or* light cream

4 eggs, beaten

1 tart apple, peeled and sliced into eighths

CRUMB MIXTURE:

5 Tbsp. butter

5 Tbsp. all-purpose flour

½ tsp. salt

2 Tbsp. brown sugar

⅔ cup chopped pecans

1. Peel and cube sweet potatoes. Place in slow cooker with water.

2. Cook on Low for 4–5 hours, until potatoes are tender.

3. Drain well and place sweet potatoes in mixing bowl.

4. Whip well with butter, salt, pepper, cardamom, sugar and evaporated milk or cream. Add eggs and beat again. (Don't add the eggs until the potatoes have been cooled off with the butter and cream, or you will have scrambled eggs!)

5. Lightly grease slow cooker. Place the mashed sweet potatoes back in the cooker and smooth top.

6. Lay apple slices on top.

7. Using two knives or a pastry cutter, cut together crumb mixture until butter pieces are at least pea-sized.

8. Sprinkle crumb topping over apple slices.

9. Cover and cook on Low for 4–5 hours. If you wish and you're around, you may remove the lid for the last 30 minutes if there is more moisture than you like.

TIP

You can assemble the dish a day or two ahead of time through step 8 and hold it in the refrigerator until ready to cook (Step 9).

Exotic Sweet Potatoes

Makes 4 servings
Prep. Time: 10–15 minutes   Cooking Time: 3–4 hours
Ideal slow-cooker size: 3-quart

1 tsp. coriander seeds

½ tsp. fennel seeds

½ tsp. dried oregano

¼ tsp. dried hot red pepper flakes

1 tsp. salt

1½ lbs. medium-sized sweet potatoes

3 Tbsp. extra-virgin olive oil

1. Coarsely grind all spices in a coffee/spice grinder. This yields a potent flavor, releasing the oils just before they're added to the other ingredients. Stir in salt.

2. Cut potatoes lengthwise into 1" wide wedges. Place them in a large mixing bowl. Toss them with the oil and spice mixture.

3. Place in slow cooker. Cover and cook on Low for 3–4 hours, until sweet potatoes are as tender as you like them.

Sweet Potato and Apple Casserole

Makes 6-8 servings

Prep. Time: 20 minutes   Cooking Time: 5¼-7¼ hours
Ideal slow-cooker size: 4- or 5-quart

⅓ cup brown sugar, firmly packed

½ tsp. ground ginger

⅛ tsp. salt

2 lbs. sweet potatoes, peeled, *divided*

2 large apples, sliced, peeled *or* not

3 Tbsp. butter, melted, *divided*

½ cup shredded coconut

¼ cup chopped pecans

1. In a small bowl combine the sugar, ginger, and salt. Set aside.
2. Cut sweet potatoes into ½"-thick slices. Put half the potatoes into your greased slow cooker.
3. Cover them with the apples.
4. Sprinkle half the brown sugar mixture over the apples.
5. Top with the rest of the sweet potato slices. Sprinkle with the remaining brown sugar mix.
6. Pour 2 Tbsp. of the melted butter over the layers.
7. Cover. Cook 5-7 hours on Low, or until the sweet potatoes are as tender as you like them.
8. Combine the coconut, pecans, and the remaining 1 Tbsp. melted butter in the small bowl. Sprinkle over the sweet potatoes and apples.
9. Cook the dish—uncovered—for 10 minutes longer.

Savory Potato Bake

Makes 8-10 servings
Prep. Time: 20 minutes ❦ Cooking Time: 3-4 hours
Ideal slow-cooker size: 5- or 6-quart

6 large potatoes,
thickly sliced, *divided*

4 medium-sized onions,
thinly sliced, *divided*

handful fresh parsley,
chopped, *divided*

salt and pepper, *divided*

5 Tbsp. butter

¼ tsp. celery seed

paprika

1. Lightly grease slow cooker. Make a layer of ⅓ of potatoes and then ¼ of onions. Sprinkle with salt and pepper and ⅓ of parsley.

2. Continue making 2 more layers and seasoning each with salt and pepper and parsley, ending with a layer of onions.

3. Place butter and celery seed in a small microwaveable dish. Heat in microwave until butter is melted.

4. Pour melted butter and celery seed over all layers in slow cooker. Sprinkle with paprika.

5. Cover and cook on High for 3-4 hours, until potatoes are tender. If there's more moisture than you like, remove the lid for the last 30 minutes and continue cooking on High.

Why I like this recipe —
   This Bake shows off the genius of the slow cooker, which gently combines these flavors and crisps up the edges to delicious effect. My favorite menu with these potatoes is grilled turkey sausages and a crisp green salad with apples and pomegranate arils.

QUICK
and
EASY

Super-Delicious Mashed Potatoes

Makes 12 servings
Prep. Time: 45 minutes ❧ Cooking Time: 2-6 hours
Ideal slow-cooker size: 5- or 6-quart

5 lbs. potatoes, peeled and cooked

2 cups milk, heated to scalding

2 Tbsp. butter, added to hot milk so it melts

8-oz. pkg. low-fat, cream cheese, softened to room temperature

1½ cups low-fat sour cream

3 tsp. onion, *or* garlic, salt

1 tsp. salt

¼–½ tsp. pepper

1. Place potatoes in mixing bowl. Beat well with mixer.

2. Add rest of ingredients and mix well.

3. Pour into slow cooker.

4. Cover. Cook on Low 2-6 hours, or until heated through, but without browning around the edges.

Cook's Note

Why the big swing in cooking time? If you've had the mashed potatoes in the fridge for several days, you may need up to 6 hours to have the middle get hot.

TIP

You can make these potatoes 3–4 days before you want to serve them. Keep them in the fridge until you want to heat and serve them.

Why I like this recipe —
The flavor is matchless. Plus you've taken away the last-minute-ness of mashed potatoes, which can stress any cook, especially if you're serving a group.

Dilly Mashed Potatoes with Spinach

Makes 6-8 servings

Prep. Time: 25 minutes 🌿 Cooking Time: 4-6 hours and then 3-4 hours

Ideal slow-cooker size: 5-quart

6 medium-sized potatoes

1 cup water

1 cup sour cream, *or* Greek yogurt, at room temperature

5 Tbsp. butter, at room temperature

4 oz. cream cheese, at room temperature

1¼ tsp. dillweed

1½ tsp. salt

⅛ tsp. pepper

2 spring onions, chopped

10-oz. box frozen chopped spinach, thawed and squeezed dry

1. Peel some or all of the potatoes. Cube. Place in slow cooker with water.

2. Cover and cook on Low for 4–6 hours, until potatoes are tender. Drain.

3. Place potatoes in mixing bowl. Add sour cream or yogurt, butter, cream cheese, dill, salt, and pepper.

4. Whip well with electric mixer.

5. Fold in spring onions and spinach.

6. Place mixture in lightly greased slow cooker, smoothing top.

7. Cook on Low for 3–4 hours.

Cheese-y Potatoes

Makes 10 servings
Prep. Time: 10-15 minutes ❦ *Cooking Time: 4¼-6¼ hours*
Ideal slow-cooker size: 5-quart

6 medium potatoes, peeled, *or*
not, and cut into ¼"-thick sticks

2 cups shredded sharp
cheddar cheese

★ 10¾-oz. can cream
of chicken soup

1 small onion, chopped

7 Tbsp. butter, melted, *divided*

1 tsp. salt

1 tsp. pepper

1 cup sour cream

2 cups seasoned stuffing cubes

★ TO MAKE YOUR OWN CREAM SOUP, SEE PAGES 370-371.

1. Toss potato sticks and cheese together in the slow cooker.

2. In a bowl, combine soup, onion, 4 Tbsp. butter, salt, and pepper. Pour over potatoes. Stir together gently.

3. Cover. Cook on Low 4-6 hours, just until the potatoes are as soft as you like them.

4. Fold in sour cream. Cover and heat for 10-15 more minutes, or just until heated through.

5. Meanwhile, toss together stuffing cubes and 3 Tbsp. butter in a bowl. Sprinkle over potatoes just before serving so the topping stays crispy.

Scalloped Potatoes Supreme

Makes 4 servings
Prep. Time: 15 minutes ❧ *Cooking Time: 4¼–5½ hours*
Ideal slow-cooker size: 4- or 5-quart

4 medium-sized potatoes, peeled and sliced into rounds, *divided*

⅓ cup chopped onion

3 tsp. all-purpose flour, *divided*

1 tsp. salt, *divided*

⅛ tsp. pepper, *divided*

1 cup cooked, diced ham

1 Tbsp. butter, minced

1⅔ cups whole milk

1 Tbsp. cornstarch

½ cup shredded sharp cheddar cheese

sprinkle of paprika

1. Arrange half of the potatoes in greased slow cooker.
2. Sprinkle with onion, 1½ tsp. flour, ½ tsp. salt, and pinch of pepper.
3. Layer remaining potatoes into dish. Top with the ham.
4. Sprinkle with remaining flour, salt, and pepper. Dot with butter.
5. Separately, whisk together the milk and cornstarch. Pour milk mixture down along one side of the inner crock so as not to disturb the seasonings and flour.
6. Cover and cook on Low for 4–5 hours. Potatoes should be almost fork-tender (poke a few, as they can vary!).
7. Sprinkle with cheese and then paprika.
8. Cook on High with lid off for 15–30 minutes, until cheese is melted and potatoes are definitely tender. Serve immediately.

Why I like this recipe —
It's a wonderful holiday side-dish that frees up my oven. It's also nice with a crunchy green salad for a light winter supper.

Gourmet Potatoes

Makes 8 servings

Prep. Time: 30 minutes ❧ Cooking Time: 4-5 hours and then 4½ hours ❧ Standing Time: 2 hours
Ideal slow-cooker size: 5-quart

8 large potatoes

2 Tbsp. olive oil

1 cup grated yellow cheddar cheese

2 Tbsp. freshly grated Parmesan

1½ cups sour cream *or* Greek yogurt

¼ cup milk

4 spring onions, chopped

1 tsp. salt

⅛ tsp. pepper

¾ cup bread crumbs

3 Tbsp. butter, melted

paprika

1. Scrub potatoes and dry well. Prick several times with a fork and rub lightly with olive oil.

2. Place oiled potatoes in slow cooker. Cover and cook on High for 4-5 hours. You want the potatoes to be cooked but still firm.

3. Remove potatoes and allow them to cool for at least an hour. Then refrigerate them for an hour. They'll grate much more easily if they're chilled through.

4. Peel the potatoes, if you wish, and then grate them.

5. In a large mixing bowl, gently mix grated potatoes, cheeses, sour cream or yogurt, milk, spring onions, salt, and pepper.

6. Spread potato mixture in lightly greased slow cooker.

7. Cover and cook on Low for 4 hours.

8. Combine bread crumbs and butter and sprinkle on top of potatoes. Sprinkle with paprika. Turn slow cooker to High. Cook uncovered for 30 minutes.

TIP

You can freeze cooked, shredded potatoes for a few weeks if you really want to get a jumpstart on your holiday menu. Otherwise, you can cook the potatoes and keep the whole potatoes in the fridge for 2–3 days.

Why I like this recipe —

This is the classic holiday side-dish for its flavor and its convenience. You can assemble the dish in your slow cooker the day before you want to serve it, and then just do steps 7-8 on the day of the meal. With this kind of convenience, I can focus on the fussier parts of the meal and still have a favorite potato dish!

Classic Stewed Tomatoes

Makes 6-8 servings
Prep. Time: 5 minutes   Cooking Time: 4½-5½ hours
Ideal slow-cooker size: 3-quart

¼ cup chopped onions

¼ cup chopped celery

2 Tbsp. butter

4 cups canned diced tomatoes, undrained

4 Tbsp. sugar

¾ tsp. salt

⅛ tsp. cinnamon

2 Tbsp. water

2 Tbsp. cornstarch

1. In a large skillet or saucepan, sauté onions and celery in butter until soft but not brown.
2. Scrape into slow cooker, being sure to get all the butter.
3. Add tomatoes, sugar, salt, and cinnamon.
4. Cover and cook on Low for 4–5 hours.
5. Combine water and cornstarch separately and whisk until smooth.
6. Whisk cornstarch mixture into hot Stewed Tomatoes until well blended.
7. Put the lid back on and cook for another 20–30 minutes on High, checking and stirring once or twice, until thickened.

Coconut Rice

Makes 6-8 servings
Prep. Time: 10 minutes ❦ Cooking Time: 2-3 hours
Ideal slow-cooker size: 3-quart

1½ cups uncooked long-grain rice

2½ cups water

1 tsp. salt

6–8 ozs. unsalted cashew halves, chopped coarsely if you don't like the bigger chunks

2 Tbsp. butter

7 ozs. flaked coconut

1 tsp. curry powder

1. Put the rice, water, and salt into your greased slow cooker. Stir them together.

2. Cover. Cook on Low for 2-3 hours, or until the liquid is fully absorbed.

3. While the rice is cooking, sauté the cashews in butter in a skillet. When they're lightly browned, add the coconut and curry powder. Stir well. Set aside.

4. When the rice is cooked, stir the cashew-coconut-curry mixture into it, using a scraper to get all the goodies out of the skillet. Then serve.

Why I like this recipe —
   I used to think rice was bland. Then I learned it didn't have to be. Rice is a good partner with coconut and curry. I'm a big nut-eater, but if you aren't wild about biting into cashew halves when you're eating rice, smash them a little before you stir them into the rice.

Rice with Peas

Makes 6 servings
Prep. Time: 20 minutes   Cooking Time: 2¼–3¼ hours
Ideal slow-cooker size: 4-quart

1½ cups long-grain white rice, uncooked

¾ cup chopped onions

2 garlic cloves, minced

★ 3⅔ cups, *or* 2 14½-oz. cans, low-fat, reduced-sodium chicken broth

⅓ cup water

¾ tsp. dried basil

½ tsp. dried oregano

½ cup frozen baby peas, thawed

¼ cup grated Parmesan cheese

★ TO MAKE YOUR OWN BROTH, SEE PAGE 357.

1. Combine rice, onions, garlic, chicken broth, water, basil, and oregano in greased slow cooker.

2. Cover. Cook on Low 2–3 hours, or until the liquid is absorbed and the rice is tender.

3. Stir in peas. Cover. Cook 15 minutes.

4. Just before serving, stir in cheese.

Colorful Rice Pilaf

Makes 10-12 servings
Prep. Time: 25 minutes ❦ Cooking Time: 2-3 hours
Ideal slow-cooker size: 5-quart

2 Tbsp. butter

2 Tbsp. peanut oil *or* vegetable oil

½ cup diced onion

1 green bell pepper, minced

3 cups uncooked long-grain rice

2 cups water

3 cups chicken broth

½ tsp. dried sage

1 tsp. poultry seasoning

few grinds pepper

¾ tsp. salt

½ cup chopped spring onions

1 cup peeled, diced, seeded fresh tomatoes

½ cup sliced green olives

½ cup sliced almonds

1. In skillet, heat butter and oil together. Add onion, pepper, and rice. Saute until vegetables are softened and rice is toasty, about 5–8 minutes.

2. Pour sauté in slow cooker.

3. Add water, broth, sage, poultry seasoning, pepper, and salt.

4. Cover and cook on Low for 2–3 hours, until rice is tender and liquid is absorbed. Turn slow cooker off.

5. Use a fork to fluff the rice and stir in the spring onions, tomatoes, and green olives. Replace lid and allow to stand for 10 minutes.

6. Meanwhile, place almonds on baking sheet. Toast in 350° oven for 3–5 minutes until almonds are fragrant and turning tan in spots.

7. Stir the almonds into Pilaf just before serving.

TIP

To peel a tomato, dip the whole tomato in boiling water for 10 seconds (it's easy to microwave a bowl of water). Run the tomato under cold water and use a paring knife or your fingers to peel off the skin. Dice it, discarding the seeds for this recipe.

Why I like this recipe —
This can be a main dish with beefy sides, or a side dish for a holiday meal. Enjoy the textures and flavors.

Green Beans in Spicy Sauce

Makes 8 servings
Prep. Time: 25 minutes   Cooking Time: 3½ hours
Ideal slow-cooker size: 4-quart

3 cups canned tomatoes
1 qt. canned green beans, drained
¼ cup diced onion
¼ cup diced celery
1 tsp. dried oregano
1 tsp. chili powder
1 Tbsp. sugar
1 bay leaf
dash red pepper
⅛ tsp. ground cloves
⅛ tsp. pepper
2 Tbsp. cornstarch
2 Tbsp. water
grated cheese for garnish, *optional*

1. Combine ingredients in slow cooker except for cornstarch, water, and grated cheese.
2. Cover and cook on Low for 3 hours.
3. Separately, mix cornstarch and water to form a smooth paste. Stir into hot mixture in slow cooker, whisking until well combined.
4. Cook on High for 20–30 minutes, stirring once or twice until thickened.
5. Garnish with grated cheese, if you wish.

Bacon and Barbecued Green Beans

Makes 4 servings

Prep. Time: 20 minutes ✂ Cooking Time: 3-8 hours
Ideal slow-cooker size: 4-quart

½ lb. bacon

4 cups whole green beans, fresh *or* frozen

¼ cup chopped onions

⅔ cup ketchup

½ cup brown sugar

3 tsp. Worcestershire sauce

¾ tsp. salt

1. Brown bacon in skillet until crisp. Lay on paper towels to drain. Reserve 2 Tbsp. bacon drippings.
2. While the bacon is crisping up, nip the stem ends off the beans, if you're using fresh ones. Wash them and shake dry. Place in slow cooker.
3. When bacon has cooled, break into pieces. Set aside.
4. Saute onions in bacon drippings in skillet.
5. Combine ketchup, brown sugar, Worcestershire sauce, and salt in skillet with sautéed onions.
6. Pour onion-ketchup mixture over green beans and mix lightly.
7. Cook on High 3-4 hours, or on Low 6-8 hours—or until the beans are as tender as you like them.
8. Stir in bacon pieces just before serving.

Eggplant Creole

Makes 4-6 servings

Prep. Time: 25 minutes   ❦   *Cooking Time: 2¼-4½ hours*

Ideal slow-cooker size: 5-quart

1 medium eggplant, unpeeled

5 Tbsp. butter, *divided*

3 Tbsp. flour

15½-oz. can petite diced tomatoes

1 small green bell pepper, chopped

1 small onion, chopped

2 garlic cloves, sliced

1 tsp. salt

1 Tbsp. brown sugar

1 bay leaf

½ tsp. ground cloves

¼ tsp. pepper

½-¾ cup bread crumbs

1. Cut the eggplant into 1" cubes. Place in greased slow cooker.

2. Melt 3 Tbsp. butter in a good-sized skillet. Add flour, stirring until smooth.

3. Then stir in the tomatoes, pepper, onion, garlic, salt, brown sugar, bay leaf, cloves, and pepper. When everything is fully blended in, let the mixture cook over medium heat for 5-10 minutes so the flavors can blend.

4. Fish out the bay leaf. Pour the rest of the ingredients over the eggplant cubes in the cooker.

5. Cover. Cook on Low for 4 hours or High for 2 hours.

6. Uncover. Scatter the bread crumbs over top of the Creole. Cut the remaining 2 Tbsp. butter into chunks and drop over the bread crumbs.

7. Let the Creole cook 5-10 more minutes, or until the butter melts and the crumbs start to brown.

Why I like this recipe—This vegetable-y mix gets all soft and saucy. There's something rich and deep going on in the slow cooker when this combination of ingredients gets together with slow, moist heat.

TIP

Eat it in a bowl with a soup spoon, or make rice and ladle the Creole over top.

Baked Corn

Makes 6 servings
Prep. Time: 15–20 minutes   ✿   Cooking Time: 4 hours
Ideal slow-cooker size: 3- or 4-quart

2 14-oz. cans creamed corn

4 eggs, beaten

1–1½ tsp. salt, according to
your taste preference

¼ tsp. pepper

2 Tbsp. sugar

half stick (4 Tbsp.) butter, melted

2 Tbsp. all-purpose flour

1½ cups milk

1. Combine everything in your greased slow cooker.
2. Cook on Low 4 hours, or until a knife inserted into the center comes out clean.

TIP

If you need to use canned corn, use the shoepeg variety. Buzz the corn and half the juice in the blender until it's partly creamed. But don't pulverize it into broth.

Rosemary Carrots

Makes 10-12 servings
Prep. Time: 15 minutes ✂ Cooking Time: 3-4 hours
Ideal slow-cooker size: 4-quart

½ lb. sweet Italian sausage, removed from casing

1 medium-sized onion, finely chopped

1–2 Tbsp. extra-virgin olive oil, *optional*

3 lbs. carrots, sliced crosswise, about ¼" thick

1 Tbsp. tomato paste

½ cup water

1 Tbsp., plus 1 tsp., chopped fresh rosemary, *or* 2 tsp. dried rosemary

salt and pepper, to taste

¼ cup chopped fresh parsley

1. In a skillet, fry together the sausage and onion. Use the olive oil if your sausage is lean and sticking to the pan. Break up clumps of sausage into small pieces.

2. Scrape sausage, onions, and any drippings into the slow cooker.

3. Stir in carrots.

4. Separately, combine tomato paste, water, rosemary, salt, and pepper. Stir into carrot mixture in the slow cooker.

5. Cover and cook on Low for 3-4 hours, depending how tender you like your carrots. Check to see if the dish needs more salt or pepper.

6. Remove carrots to serving dish, sprinkling with parsley.

Broccoli, Corn, and Onion Gratin

Makes 6 servings

Prep. Time: 20 minutes 💥 Cooking Time: 2-3 hours
Ideal slow-cooker size: 4-quart

1½ cups chopped broccoli

2 cups creamed corn

2 eggs, slightly beaten

★ ½ cup plain yogurt

1 Tbsp. flour

1 tsp. seasoned salt

1 cup French-fried onions, *divided*

★ TO MAKE YOUR OWN YOGURT, SEE PAGE 368.

1. Place broccoli in greased slow cooker.

2. In a mixing bowl, combine corn, eggs, yogurt, flour, and seasoned salt.

3. Pour half of the corn mixture over broccoli.

4. Sprinkle with ½ cup onions.

5. Pour rest of corn mixture over onions. Sprinkle remaining ½ cup onions on top.

6. Cover and cook on Low for 2-3 hours, until set and broccoli is tender.

Southern-Style Greens

Makes 6-8 servings
Prep. Time: 25 minutes ❦ *Cooking Time: 8-10 hours*
Ideal slow-cooker size: 6-quart

1 large bunch collard greens, about 2 lbs., to yield 5-6 quarts loosely-packed chopped greens

1 small smoked ham hock

pinch red pepper flakes, *or more if you like*

a few grinds of freshly ground pepper

2 cups water

1 Tbsp. balsamic vinegar, *or more if you like*

TIP

You can use kale for this recipe, too. Swiss chard and turnip greens can be part of the mix, but they don't need the long cooking that kale and collards can handle.

1. To prepare the collards, rinse the leaves. Strip the leaves off the tough stems. Discard stems. Stack several leaves together and roll them up. Use a large, sharp knife to cut them into ½" ribbons. You should have 5-6 quarts of chopped greens, loosely packed.

2. Combine chopped greens, ham hock, red pepper, pepper, and water in slow cooker. The greens will be fluffy and right up against the lid, but they will cook down.

3. Cover and cook on Low for 8-10 hours, stirring once in the middle of the cooking time if you're around. The greens should have cooked down to a surprisingly small heap and should be quite soft.

4. Remove ham hock to cutting board. Hold it still with a fork and use a knife to cut and shred the meat off the bone.

5. Return the meat to the greens. Stir in vinegar. Taste for salt and heat. Serve hot.

Why I like this recipe —

I learned how to make greens when big, vibrant bunches of them started appearing in market in the fall. I talked to a Southern cook and learned the traditional stovetop method, but boy, the slow cooker does make it easy to cook the greens! Apparently, Southern cooks steep hot peppers in white vinegar for months and add this "pepper oil" to the greens at the end. I simply use some red pepper flakes and vinegar.

Baked Herb Spinach

Makes 4 servings
Prep. Time: 20 minutes   Cooking Time: 2-3 hours
Ideal slow-cooker size: 3-quart

1 lb. fresh spinach, chopped, *or* 10-oz. pkg. frozen spinach, thawed and squeezed dry

2 eggs, beaten

½ cup milk

1 cup grated cheddar cheese

1 cup cooked rice

¼ cup chopped onion

2 Tbsp. butter

½ tsp. Worcestershire sauce

1 tsp. salt

1½ tsp. chopped fresh thyme, *or* ½ tsp. dried

1. Mix all ingredients together in your greased slow cooker.

2. Cover. Cook on Low 2 hours.

3. Gently shake the cooker to see if the mixture is jiggly or set. If it's jiggly, especially in the middle, cover the cooker and cook another 30 minutes. Check again. Cover and cook another 20-30 minutes until it's set, but not drying around the edges.

Party Walnut Broccoli

QUICK
and
EASY

Makes 8-10 servings

Prep. Time: 15-20 minutes ❦ Cooking Time: 5-6 hours
Ideal slow-cooker size: 4- or 5-quart

2 lbs. fresh broccoli,
trimmed and cut
into florets

6 Tbsp. butter,
melted, *divided*

4 Tbsp. flour

★ 1 cup chicken broth

1 cup skim milk

⅔ cup water

2 cups herb stuffing

⅔ cup chopped walnuts

★ TO MAKE YOUR OWN BROTH, SEE PAGE 357.

1. Put broccoli into your greased slow cooker.

2. Stir in 2 Tbsp. butter, the flour, chicken broth, and milk. Mix together well.

3. Heat the water in a microwave-safe bowl in the microwave. Stir in the remaining 4 Tbsp. melted butter.

4. Pour over the stuffing in a good-sized bowl. Add the walnuts. Toss to mix evenly.

5. Spoon the moistened stuffing and walnuts over the broccoli.

6. Cover. Cook on Low 5-6 hours. Take the lid off during the last 30 minutes to let the stuffing crisp up a bit.

Cheesy Broccoli Bake

Makes 4-6 servings
Prep. Time: 20 minutes ❧ Cooking Time: 2½-3½ hours
Ideal slow-cooker size: 4-quart

3 eggs

2 Tbsp. flour

4 oz. cottage cheese

1½ cups (6 ozs.) cheddar cheese, grated

1 tsp. dried oregano

¾ tsp. dried basil

⅛ tsp. pepper

3 cups small broccoli florets

2 Tbsp. butter, melted

½ cup bread crumbs

2 Tbsp. freshly grated Parmesan cheese

1. In a mixing bowl, beat eggs and flour until smooth.

2. Beat in cottage cheese, cheddar cheese, oregano, basil, and pepper.

3. Place broccoli florets in lightly greased slow cooker. Pour cheese mixture over them.

4. Cover and cook on High for 2-3 hours, until broccoli is tender and casserole is set.

5. Separately, combine butter, bread crumbs, and Parmesan.

6. Sprinkle over top of casserole. Cook uncovered for 20 minutes on High.

Why I like this recipe — This Bake is a potluck winner every time. It's recognizable (broccoli, cheese, bread crumbs) and it's comfort food. Vegetarians will be happy to have a meatless option, and you will be happy to take an empty cooker home!

Summer Squash Casserole

Makes 6-8 servings
Prep. Time: 25 minutes ❧ *Cooking Time: 2½ hours*
Ideal slow-cooker size: 3-quart

5 medium-sized summer squash, peeled or not, sliced

1 tomato, chopped

3 spring onions, sliced

¼ tsp. freshly ground pepper

2 eggs, beaten

½ cup milk

½ tsp. salt

1½ cups grated cheddar, *or* Monterey Jack, cheese

½ cup chopped fresh basil

2 Tbsp. butter, melted

2 Tbsp. freshly grated Parmesan cheese

½ cup Italian bread crumbs

1. Gently mix the squash, tomato, onion, and pepper in lightly greased slow cooker.

2. Separately, combine eggs, milk, salt, and cheese in a mixing bowl.

3. Pour egg mixture over squash. Cover and cook on High for 2 hours, or until set.

4. Sprinkle with basil.

5. Combine melted butter with Parmesan and bread crumbs. Sprinkle over basil layer in slow cooker.

6. Keep slow cooker on High with lid off and cook an additional 20 minutes.

Why I like this recipe —
   Adding the basil to an old familiar squash casserole yields wonderful summer flavor.
I hope you enjoy it! It's a great summer supper with corn on the cob (isn't everything?).

Baked Lima Beans

Makes 10-12 servings

Prep. Time: 5 minutes ❧ *Soaking Time: 8 hours, or overnight* ❧ *Cooking Time: 11-13 hours*

Ideal slow-cooker size: 4-quart

1 lb. dry lima beans

2½ cups water

½ cup minced onion

¾ cup chopped celery

¾ cup mild molasses (not blackstrap)

½ cup brown sugar

½ cup ketchup

1½ tsp. dry mustard

1½ tsp. salt

1½ cups tomato juice

1½ Tbsp. Worcestershire sauce

¼ tsp. pepper

½ lb. bacon

1. Wash beans, making sure you get rid of any hulls or stones. Pour them into your slow cooker. Cover them with water that comes at least 2″ above the beans. Cover the cooker and soak the beans for 8 hours or overnight.

2. Pour off the soaking water. Add 2½ cups fresh water.

3. Stir in all of the ingredients except the bacon.

4. Cover. Cook on Low 11-13 hours, or until the beans are tender.

5. While the bean mixture is cooking, fry the bacon until crisp. Remove from the drippings and place on a paper-towel-covered plate to drain. Then break the bacon into pieces. Set aside until nearly the end of the cooking time.

6. Fifteen minutes before the beans finish cooking, stir in the bacon pieces.

Why I like this recipe —
Sometimes I get the urge for baked beans that have some real fiber and personality. These don't demand a lot of the cook. They're just after long, slow cooking. And they reward richly at your next potluck or picnic. Or make a pot on Saturday and keep them in the fridge to round out the upcoming week's meals.

Country French Vegetables

Makes 4-5 servings
Prep. Time: 10 minutes ✽ Cooking Time: 3-6 hours
Ideal slow-cooker size: 5-quart

3 Tbsp. extra-virgin olive oil, *divided*

3 potatoes, unpeeled, cut in 1" pieces

2 carrots, unpeeled, cut in 1" pieces

1 parsnip, peeled, cut in 1" pieces

1 turnip *or* rutabaga, peeled, cut in 1" pieces

2 onions, cut in wedges

½ lb. fresh mushrooms, halved

1 Tbsp. minced fresh, *or* ½ tsp. dried, rosemary

1 Tbsp. minced fresh, *or* ½ tsp. dried, thyme

⅓ cup chopped fresh parsley

¾ tsp. salt

¼ tsp. freshly ground black pepper

1. Lightly grease slow cooker with 1 Tbsp. olive oil.

2. Combine all ingredients with remaining 2 Tbsp. olive oil in slow cooker

3. Cover and cook on Low for 3-6 hours, depending how tender you want the vegetables or how long you want to be away from home.

TIP
Rutabagas are usually milder and sweeter than turnips, and if you're doubtful, you can leave them out.

Why I like this recipe —
It's a straightforward winter
vegetable dish, and I like shopping for rutabagas
at market and discussing them with the farmers.

Zucchini Almondine

Makes 6 servings
Prep. Time: 20-30 minutes   ✂   Cooking Time: 3¼-4¼ hours
Ideal slow-cooker size: 3-quart

4 cups grated zucchini,
peeled *or* unpeeled

1¼ cups cheese, grated, your
choice of flavors, *divided*

1 cup bread crumbs

¾ cup chopped onion

¼ tsp. garlic powder

3 Tbsp. butter

1 tsp. salt

¼ tsp. pepper

½ cup milk

2 eggs

½ cup slivered almonds

1. Combine zucchini, 1 cup of cheese, bread crumbs, onions, garlic powder, butter, salt, and pepper in your greased slow cooker.

2. Combine the milk and eggs in a bowl. Then pour the mixture over the zucchini, and stir everything together.

3. Cover. Cook on Low 3-4 hours, or until the zucchini is as tender as you like it.

4. Sprinkle with the remaining cheese and almonds. Turn the cooker to High, keep the lid off, and cook for 10-15 minutes, or until the cheese melts.

Fast and Fabulous Brussels Sprouts

Makes 4-6 servings
Prep. Time: 15 minutes ❧ Cooking Time: 2-5 hours
Ideal slow-cooker size: 2- or 3-quart

1 lb. Brussels sprouts, bottoms trimmed off and halved

3 Tbsp. butter, melted

1½ Tbsp. Dijon mustard

¼ tsp. salt

¼ tsp. freshly ground black pepper

¼ cup water

½ tsp. dried tarragon, *optional*

TIP
The flavor goes so well with so many meals: any autumnal meal with baked squash, Easter ham, pasta dishes, chicken and rice, and more.

1. Mix all ingredients in slow cooker.

2. Cover and cook on High for 2-2½ hours, or Low for 4-5 hours, until sprouts are just soft. Some of the Brussels sprouts at the sides will get brown and crispy, and this is delicious.

3. Stir well to distribute sauce. Serve hot or warm.

Why I like this recipe —
These Brussels sprouts are just so delicious that I think you can convert sprouts-haters with a bite. I've seen my family snitch these sprouts out of the serving dish after the meal was over, so one time I served them at room temperature on purpose. Fabulous, indeed!

Festive Squash

Makes 8 servings
Prep. Time: 20 minutes ✂ Cooking Time: 4–5 hours
Ideal slow-cooker size: 3-quart

4 cups cubed butternut, *or* other winter squash, *divided*

½ tsp. salt, *divided*

pinch pepper, *divided*

2 apples, cored and thinly sliced, *divided*

¼ cup raisins, *divided*

⅓ cup orange juice, *or* apple juice, *or* apple cider

2 Tbsp. butter

¼ cup chopped, toasted walnuts

TIP
Stir 1 Tbsp. grated orange rind into juice.

1. Place half the squash in lightly greased slow cooker. Season with salt and pepper.
2. Follow with a layer of half the apples and raisins.
3. Repeat the layers.
4. Pour juice over all. Dot with butter.
5. Cover and cook on Low for 4–5 hours, until squash is tender when pricked with a fork.
6. Sprinkle with walnuts just before serving.

Southern Cornbread Dressing

Makes 4 servings

Prep. Time: 30 minutes ❧ Cooking Time: 4-5 hours

Ideal slow-cooker size: 3-quart

1 cup chopped onion

1 cup chopped celery

¼ cup (half stick) butter

2 cups crumbled cornbread

⅓ cup chopped walnuts

1 cup applesauce

½ tsp. poultry seasoning

½ tsp. dried thyme

½ tsp. dried sage

¼ cup chopped fresh parsley

1. In a skillet, sauté onion and celery in butter until softened.

2. Scrape into mixing bowl, being sure not to leave any butter behind.

3. Spread crumbled cornbread on baking sheet. Spread walnuts on another baking sheet. Bake in 350° oven until walnuts are fragrant and just turning tan (7–10 minutes) and cornbread is toasty (10-15 minutes).

4. Pour cornbread and walnuts into lightly greased slow cooker with celery and onion.

5. Add rest of ingredients and mix gently. Taste to see if it needs salt, which varies according to the cornbread you're using.

6. Cover. Cook on Low for 4–5 hours.

TIP

This recipe is handy for holidays to free up oven space. You can toast the nuts and cornbread at least a day ahead of time.

Why I like this recipe —
I love this recipe for any leftover cornbread, which I confess I like best freshly made. This is a delicious transformation!

Moist Stuffing

Makes 10 servings
Prep. Time: 30 minutes ❧ Cooking Time: 5 hours
Standing Time: 8-12 hours if you need to dry out the bread
Ideal slow-cooker size: 5-quart

12 cups cubed, hearty bread

4 ribs celery, chopped

2 medium onions, chopped

¼ cup (half stick) butter

¼ cup minced fresh parsley

2 tsp. poultry seasoning

½ tsp. dried sage

2 eggs

★ 3-4 cups stock, chicken *or* vegetable

★ TO MAKE YOUR OWN STOCK, SEE PAGES 357-358

1. The bread should be dried out and stale for the best texture in the finished dressing. You can leave the bread cubes sitting out for 8-12 hours, or you can lightly toast them in a 350° oven for 10-15 minutes. Set aside.

2. In a skillet, sauté together the celery and onions in butter.

3. Pour sauté into mixing bowl, being sure to get all the butter.

4. Add the rest of the ingredients, starting with only 3 cups stock. Depending on how dry your bread was, you may want to add as much as another cup of stock. Mix the ingredients thoroughly.

5. Place dressing mixture in greased slow cooker, smoothing top.

6. Cover and cook on Low 5 hours.

Why I like this recipe —
This is a clever feat at the holidays when you are juggling oven and stovetop space. Just fill up your slow cooker with this stuffing, even the day before if you put it in the fridge, and put the cooker off in a quiet corner to cook. We all like shortcuts for holiday meals! I think you'll love the flavor of this classic stuffing, too.

Potluck Baked Beans

QUICK and EASY

Makes 5 servings
Prep. Time: 15 minutes ❦ *Cooking Time: 4–8 hours*
Ideal slow-cooker size: 4-quart

6 slices bacon

1 cup chopped onion

3 11-oz. cans pork and beans, 2 cans drained and 1 undrained

⅓ cup brown sugar

1 Tbsp. blackstrap molasses

1 Tbsp. apple cider vinegar

1 apple, chopped

1 Tbsp. prepared mustard

1½ tsp. Worcestershire sauce

½ cup ketchup

dash hot sauce

1. Saute onion and bacon together in skillet until brown.

2. Scrape the onion and bacon into slow cooker. Health-conscious people might drain off some bacon drippings.

3. Add rest of ingredients and stir well.

4. Cook on Low for 4–8 hours. The beans get good with a long or short cooking time, so make your potluck plans freely.

Why I like this recipe —
Baked beans are the backbone of potlucks and picnics around here. I like how flexible the cooking time is in this recipe, so I can take it to a potluck at noon after church or to an evening picnic.

Best-in-the-West Beans

Makes 8-10 servings
Prep. Time: 30 minutes ❦ *Cooking Time: 5 hours*
Ideal slow-cooker size: 5-quart

½ lb. ground beef

10 slices bacon, chopped

½ cup onion, chopped

⅓ cup brown sugar

⅓ cup white sugar

¼ cup ketchup

¼ cup barbecue sauce

2 Tbsp. prepared mustard

2 Tbsp. molasses

½ tsp. salt

½ tsp. chili powder

½ tsp. pepper

1-lb. can kidney beans, rinsed and drained

1-lb. can butter beans, rinsed and drained

1-lb. can pork and beans, undrained

1. Brown the ground beef and bacon together in a skillet. Lift the meat out of the skillet with a slotted spoon so drippings stay behind. Put the meat into your greased slow cooker.

2. Add the onions to the meat drippings. Cook them just until they soften a little. Add them to the meat in the slow cooker.

3. Stir all of the other ingredients into the slow cooker. Combine everything well.

4. Cover. Cook on High for 1 hour. Reduce heat to Low and cook for 4 more hours.

Why I like this recipe —

This is a grand baked bean recipe. Okay, there are a bunch of ingredients, but apart from browning the beef, bacon, and onions, all you need to do is dig the rest of the goodies out of your cupboard, measure them, and stir them into your cooker. Put these on to cook before you go to your child's game or the pool, or turn them on mid-morning at your campsite.

Breads

Delicious Blueberry Bread

Makes 1 8" loaf

Prep. Time: 15 minutes ❦ *Cooking Time: 3½–4 hours* ❦ *Standing Time: 15 minutes*
Ideal slow-cooker size: 6-quart oval

1 egg

⅔ cup sugar

2 Tbsp. vegetable oil

⅔ cup orange juice

½ tsp. grated orange rind

1½ cups all-purpose flour

½ cup whole wheat flour

1½ tsp. baking powder

½ tsp. baking soda

½ tsp. salt

1 cup fresh, *or* frozen, blueberries, thawed

1. Place egg in large mixing bowl and beat well.

2. Add sugar, oil, orange juice, and orange rind, and continue beating till well mixed.

3. In a separate bowl, sift together flours, baking powder, baking soda, and salt. Add to wet ingredients. Mix only a few strokes until barely combined.

4. Gently stir in blueberries. Do not overmix.

5. Pour into well-greased 8 × 4 loaf pan, or whatever size loaf pan fits in your slow cooker. You can also use small, individual bakers.

6. Place pan or bakers into dry inner crock on top of a small trivet or 2 metal jar rings. Prop lid open at one end with a chopstick or wooden spoon handle. Cook for 3½–4 hours on High, or until toothpick inserted in middle of loaf comes out clean. The top of the loaf may not look set because it won't brown the way it would in the oven, so be sure to start checking at 3½ hours.

7. Carefully remove hot loaf pan or bakers from hot cooker and let bread cool in the pan or bakers at least 15 minutes. Run a table knife around the loaf and carefully turn pan upside down.

8. Serve slices warm with butter or whipped cream cheese.

TIP

You may use up to 1 cup of whole wheat flour in this bread without sacrificing the nice, moist texture.

Healthy Pumpkin Bread

Makes 1 loaf

Prep. Time: 25 minutes ❧ *Cooking Time: 3½–4 hours* ❧ *Standing Time: 10 minutes*
Ideal slow-cooker size: 6-quart

⅓ cup oil

1 cup honey

2 eggs

1 cup cooked pumpkin

2 Tbsp. water

⅓ cup raisins

⅓ cup nuts

1½ cups + 2 Tbsp. whole wheat flour

¼ tsp. baking powder

1 tsp. baking soda

½ tsp. salt

½ tsp. ground cinnamon

¼ tsp. ground ginger

¼ tsp. ground cloves

1. In a small mixing bowl, mix oil, honey, eggs, pumpkin, water, raisins, and nuts.

2. In a larger mixing bowl, mix rest of ingredients.

3. Add the wet ingredients to the dry, stirring briefly, just until mixed.

4. Pour into greased 9 × 5 or 8 × 4 loaf pan, whatever size will fit in your slow cooker.

5. Place loaf pan on small trivet or metal jar rings in slow cooker. Prop lid open at one end with a wooden spoon handle or chopstick.

6. Cook on High for 3½–4 hours, until tester inserted in middle of loaf comes out clean.

7. Carefully, wearing oven mitts, remove hot loaf pan from hot crock. Allow to cool for 10 minutes, then run a knife around the edge of the loaf and turn out onto cooling rack. Wait as long as you can, at least 10 minutes, before slicing.

Zucchini Bread

Makes 1 loaf

Prep. Time: 20 minutes ❦ *Cooking Time: 3½–4 hours* ❦ *Standing Time: 40 minutes*
Ideal slow-cooker size: 6-quart oval

1 cup whole wheat flour

2 cups all-purpose flour

1½ cups sugar

1 tsp. cinnamon

1 tsp. salt

1 tsp. baking powder

1 tsp. baking soda

2 cups shredded, unpeeled zucchini

1 cup chopped nuts

1 cup raisins, *or* dried cranberries, *or* some of both

★ **¾ cup plain yogurt**

¾ cup oil

★ TO MAKE YOUR OWN YOGURT, SEE PAGE 368.

1. In a mixing bowl, combine both flours, sugar, cinnamon, salt, baking powder, and baking soda.

2. In another bowl, combine zucchini, nuts, raisins, yogurt, and oil.

3. Pour the wet ingredients into the dry. Mix briefly and carefully just until mixed—streaks of flour are okay. Overmixed quick breads are tough!

4. Pour batter into greased loaf pan, whatever size will fit in your slow cooker. Place a trivet or metal jar rings in the bottom of the slow cooker and place loaf pan on it.

5. Vent slow cooker lid at one end by propping it open with a wooden spoon handle or chopstick.

6. Cook on High for 3½–4 hours, until tester inserted in middle of loaf comes out clean.

7. Carefully, wearing oven mitts, remove hot loaf pan from hot cooker. Allow to cool for 10 minutes, then run a knife around the edge of the pan and turn loaf out onto rack. Cool for at least 30 more minutes before slicing.

Cranberry Almond Bread

Makes 1 loaf

Prep. Time: 20 minutes ❧ *Cooking Time: 3½–4 hours* ❧ *Standing Time: 10 minutes*
Ideal slow-cooker size: 6-quart

2 cups all-purpose flour

¾ cup brown sugar

1½ tsp. baking powder

½ tsp. baking soda

1 tsp. salt

4 Tbsp. (half stick) butter, melted

1 egg

¾ cup milk

½ tsp. almond extract

1 cup fresh cranberries

½ cup sliced almonds

1. In a mixing bowl, mix flour, sugar, baking powder, baking soda, and salt.

2. In another bowl, combine butter, egg, milk, and almond extract. When well-mixed, add cranberries and almonds.

3. Combine wet and dry mixtures, stirring lightly and carefully until just mixed.

4. Spread batter (it will be stiff) in greased loaf 9 × 5 or 8 × 4 pan, whatever size fits into your slow cooker.

5. Place pan on small trivet or metal jar lid/rings in bottom of slow cooker. Vent slow cooker lid at one end with a wooden spoon or chopstick.

6. Cook on High for 3½–4 hours, until tester inserted in middle of loaf comes out clean.

7. Carefully, wearing oven mitts, remove hot pan from hot cooker. Allow to stand for 10 minutes. Run a knife around the edge and turn out loaf to finish cooling on cooling rack. Slice when cool.

TIP

Whole milk will give the best moisture and texture in this recipe.

Why I like this recipe —
Sure, cranberries pair beautifully with oranges and I love that combination, but putting cranberries with not-too-sweet almond bread is a revelation. A slice of this bread with a cup of hot chocolate is one of my favorite Thanksgiving-is-coming treats.

Why I like this recipe—
I love strawberries and this is a uniquely delicious way to use them. Sometimes I just can't help myself and I put a drop of red food coloring in the icing.

Festive Strawberry Loaf

Makes 1 loaf
Prep. Time: 20 minutes ❦ Cooking Time: 3½–4 hours
Ideal slow-cooker size: 6-quart oval

1 cup all-purpose flour

½ cup whole wheat flour

¾ cup sugar

½ tsp. baking soda

¼ tsp. salt

½ tsp. cinnamon

2 eggs

½ cup + 2 Tbsp. vegetable oil

1 cup chopped fresh, *or* frozen and thawed, strawberries

FROSTING:

4 oz. cream cheese, softened

½ tsp. vanilla

4 Tbsp. (half-stick) butter, softened

1¼ cups confectioners sugar

chopped pecans, *optional*

1. In a large bowl, combine both flours, sugar, baking soda, salt, and cinnamon. When well mixed, form a well in the center of the mixture.

2. In a separate bowl, beat eggs and vegetable oil. Add strawberries. Pour into well in dry ingredients and stir gently just until mixed.

3. Pour into well-greased 8 × 4 loaf pan or whatever size fits in your slow cooker.

4. Place pan into inner crock on top of a small trivet or metal jar lid. Prop lid open at one end with a chopstick or wooden spoon handle.

5. Cook for 3½–4 hours on High, or until toothpick inserted in middle of loaf comes out clean. The top of the loaf may not look set because it won't brown the way it would in the oven, so be sure to start checking at 3½ hours.

6. Carefully remove hot loaf pan and let bread cool in the pan at least 15 minutes. Run a table knife around the loaf and carefully turn pan upside down to get loaf out.

7. To make the frosting, beat cream cheese, vanilla, and butter together until creamy in a medium-sized bowl. Stir in confectioners sugar.

8. Spread frosting over top and part of the way down the sides of the cooled bread. Sprinkle evenly with pecans if you're using them and press in lightly.

TIP

This bread freezes well.

Special Banana Bread

Makes 1 loaf

Prep. Time: 20 minutes ❧ *Cooking Time: 3½–4½ hours* ❧ *Standing Time: 10 minutes*
Ideal slow-cooker size: 6-quart

1⅓ cups all-purpose flour

⅔ cup whole wheat flour

¾ tsp. baking soda

½ tsp. salt

1 cup mashed, very ripe banana (2–3 medium)

½ cup creamy peanut butter

½ cup sugar

⅓ cup buttermilk

⅓ cup vegetable oil

2 eggs

1 tsp. vanilla extract

1 cup semisweet chocolate chips

1. In a mixing bowl, combine flours, baking soda, and salt.
2. In another mixing bowl, stir together banana, peanut butter, sugar, buttermilk, oil, eggs, and vanilla. When well-mixed, stir in chocolate chips.
3. Add wet ingredients to dry (or the other way around) and be very careful to stir briefly until just mixed. A few streaks of flour may remain.
4. Pour batter in greased loaf pan, 9 × 5 or 8 × 4, whatever size fits in your cooker. Or use small, individual bakers.
5. Place loaf pan or bakers on metal jar rings or small trivet in cooker. Prop slow cooker lid open at one end with a wooden spoon handle or chopstick.
6. Cook on High for 3½–4½ hours, until tester inserted in middle comes out clean.
7. Carefully, wearing oven gloves, remove the hot loaf pan or bakers from the hot cooker. Allow to stand for 10 minutes. Run a knife around the edge of the bread and turn the loaf out onto a wire rack to finish cooling. Slices best when cool, if you can wait that long!

Why I like this recipe —
    What's better than banana, peanut butter, and chocolate? I love these three together. This is a wonderfully flavored bread that you don't have to feel guilty eating—serve it for breakfast or an after-school snack. I usually eat it straight up, but you could spread cream cheese on it, too.

Yeasted Cornbread

Makes 1 loaf

Prep. Time: 30 minutes ❧ *Standing Time: 30 minutes* ❧ *Cooking Time: 2½–3 hours*
Ideal slow-cooker size: 6-quart oval

¾ cup boiling water

½ cup yellow cornmeal

¼ cup shortening

3 Tbsp. mild molasses, *or* honey

1 tsp. salt

1 pkg. (1 Tbsp.) dry yeast

¼ cup warm water

1 egg

1 cup whole wheat flour

1½ cups all-purpose flour, preferably unbleached

TIP

Use this bread anywhere you would use regular cornbread.

1. In a mixing bowl, pour boiling water over cornmeal, shortening, molasses and salt. Stir until shortening melts. Allow to cool to room temperature, at least 30 minutes.

2. When the cornmeal mixture is just lukewarm, add yeast, warm water, and egg. Whisk well.

3. Using hands or a wooden spoon, stir in whole wheat flour and all-purpose flour. The dough will be thick and unwieldy. Knead a few turns if you wish, but it's not necessary.

4. Shape dough into loaf and place in well-greased bread pan, whichever size will fit in your slow cooker.

5. Place bread pan on a small trivet or metal jar lid in inner crock. Lay 4 paper towels on top of crock (to catch the condensation). Put lid on slow cooker, right on top of the paper towels.

6. Cook on High for 2½–3 hours, until the middle top of the loaf springs back when touched and the whole loaf has pulled away from the sides of the pan and is lightly brown. The loaf may not puff up in the middle completely.

7. Carefully remove hot loaf pan from hot crock. Run a knife around the loaf and turn it out onto a rack to finish cooling. Delicious sliced and served warm, or toasted the next morning for breakfast.

Cornbread from Scratch

Makes 6 servings
Prep. Time: 15 minutes ❦ Cooking Time: 2-3 hours
Ideal slow-cooker size: 2- or 3-quart

1 cup flour

1 cup yellow cornmeal

4½ tsp. baking powder

1 tsp. salt

1 egg, slightly beaten

2 Tbsp. honey

1 cup milk

⅓ cup melted butter, *or* oil

½ tsp. orange liqueur

1. Cut a piece of parchment paper to cover the bottom of the inner crock, and then put it in the crock. Spray the inside of the crock, including the parchment paper.

2. In a mixing bowl sift together the flour, cornmeal, baking powder, and salt. Make a well in the center.

3. In a separate bowl, stir together egg, honey, milk, butter, and orange liqueur until well mixed. Pour into well in dry ingredients.

4. Mix into the dry mixture until just moistened. Spread out with a spoon or spatula so the batter covers the bottom of the crock evenly.

5. Cover. Cook on High 2-3 hours, or until tester inserted into center of bread comes out clean.

TIP
When you lift the lid, swoop it off at a sharp angle so no water drips off the inside of the lid onto the cake.

Why I like this recipe —
This is so easy and so tasty, you don't really need a boxed mix to make your own cornbread. Just make sure to pick up some cornmeal the next time you're in the grocery store. And some orange liqueur, too, although you can skip that if you get a sudden urge to make this and don't have it on hand. It's there as a subtle hint, not to over-power the bread.

Moist Cornbread

QUICK and EASY

Makes 12 servings
Prep. Time: 10-15 minutes 🌿 Cooking Time: 1½-2½ hours
Ideal slow-cooker size: 3-quart

¾ cup yellow cornmeal

1 cup whole wheat flour

1 tsp. baking soda

1 tsp. cream of tartar

1 tsp. salt

3 Tbsp. sugar

1 egg

★ 1 cup sour cream,
or plain yogurt

½ cup milk

3 Tbsp. butter, melted

★ TO MAKE YOUR OWN YOGURT, SEE PAGE 368

1. Mix cornmeal, flour, baking soda, cream of tartar, salt, and sugar in a mixing bowl.
2. In a separate bowl, beat egg well, and then add sour cream or yogurt, milk, and melted butter. Mix well.
3. Pour wet ingredients into flour mixture. Stir just until mixed.
4. Pour into greased slow cooker.
5. Cook on High for 1½-2½ hours or until tester inserted in middle comes out clean.

Cook's Note —

- *For breakfast, serve the Cornbread with sausage gravy and fried apples on the side.*

- *For a main meal, serve it with smoked sausage, steamed cabbage, pinto beans, and applesauce.*

TIP
Leftovers can be split into pieces, buttered lightly, and placed under the broiler until browned. Delicious!

Why I like this recipe —
The slow cooker makes a whole-grain cornbread moist and delicious. Dry cornbread is terrible stuff to have in your mouth, but this recipe will keep you coming back for more!

Maple-Nut Cornbread with Country Bacon

Makes 1 loaf

Prep. Time: 20 minutes ❦ Cooking Time: 2 hours
Ideal slow-cooker size: 3-quart

6 strips double-smoked, *or regular if you can't find this high-octane kind*, bacon

1 cup yellow cornmeal

½ cup all-purpose flour

1 tsp. baking soda

1 tsp. baking powder

1 tsp. salt

¼ cup maple syrup

½ cup buttermilk

¼ cup vegetable oil

2 eggs

½ cup pecans, coarsely chopped

vanilla yogurt, *or* maple syrup for topping, *optional*

1. Fry the bacon over medium heat in a skillet. When the bacon is crisp, reserve the drippings and remove the bacon to drain on a paper towel. Then crumble the bacon into chunks.

2. Combine the cornmeal, flour, baking soda, baking powder, and salt in a good-sized bowl.

3. In a separate bowl, beat together the maple syrup, buttermilk, oil, and eggs.

4. Stir the liquid mixture into the dry ingredients. Mix well.

5. Combine the pecans with the crumbled bacon. Stir them into the batter.

6. Pour just enough reserved bacon drippings into your greased slow cooker to coat the bottom with a thin film. Then pour the batter into the cooker.

7. Cover. Cook the Bread on High for 2 hours, or until a toothpick inserted in center of cake comes out clean.

8. Serve warm. Vanilla yogurt or maple syrup makes a good topping.

Why I like this recipe—
This has got texture, plus a mix of salty and sweet that makes me want to eat this bread straight out of the cooker. This is good brunch food, or stick a wedge in your lunch. It's also a good go-along with chili or soup.

Mexican-Style Cornbread

Makes 12-15 servings
Prep. Time: 20 minutes ✽ Cooking Time: 2½–3 hours
Ideal slow-cooker size: 4-quart

3 cups yellow cornmeal

1½ tsp. baking powder

2 tsp. salt

1 cup chopped onion

1 cup cream-style corn

4-oz. can chopped
green chilies, drained

1¼ cups grated sharp
cheddar cheese

1 cup vegetable oil

3 eggs, beaten

1¾ cups milk

paprika

1. In large mixing bowl, combine cornmeal, baking powder, and salt. Mix in onion, corn, chilies, and cheese.

2. In a separate bowl, mix together oil, eggs, and milk. Pour wet ingredients into cornmeal mixture and blend gently just until mixed.

3. Spoon mixture into greased slow cooker. Sprinkle with paprika.

4. Cook on High for 2½–3 hours, until tester inserted in middle comes out clean.

5. Serve by spooning out portions (the fast, but not pretty, method), or run knife around the edges and invert crock over cutting board to get bread out. Slice.

Southwest Cornbread

Makes 1 loaf

Prep. Time: 15–20 minutes ❦ Cooking Time: 2–3 hours
Ideal slow-cooker size: 6-quart oval

1 cup cornmeal

1 cup all-purpose flour

1 Tbsp. baking powder

½ tsp. salt, *optional*

2 Tbsp. chopped
fresh cilantro

1 egg, beaten

1 cup milk

1 cup creamed corn

1 small onion, chopped

1–2 jalapeño peppers,
seeded and minced,
depending on how
much you like heat

half stick (¼ cup) butter

½ cup grated
cheddar cheese

1. In a good-sized bowl, mix together the cornmeal, flour, baking powder, salt if you want, and cilantro.

2. In a separate bowl, mix together the egg, milk, and corn until thoroughly combined.

3. In a small skillet, or in a microwave-safe bowl, cook the onion and jalapeño in butter until the onion is transparent.

4. Add the milk mixture, the onion mixture, and the cheese to the dry ingredients. Stir until just mixed.

5. Pour into a 2-qt. greased baking pan if it fits into your slow cooker. Or use an 8 × 4 loaf pan if it fits into your cooker.

6. Cover the baking pan securely with tin foil. Put the lid on the slow cooker.

Cook on High 2–3 hours, or until a toothpick inserted into the center of the bread comes out clean.

TIP

The baking pan doesn't need to sit the whole way on the bottom of your cooker. If the cooker holds the pan level, it's okay to have it hang on the edges of the crock.

Why I like this recipe—
I love the zing in this innocent-looking bread. And you won't heat up your kitchen if you make the bread in your slow cooker.

Whole Wheat Oatmeal Bread

Makes 1 loaf
Prep. Time: 30 minutes   ✻   Cooking Time: 2½–3 hours
Ideal slow-cooker size: 6-quart

1 Tbsp. (1 pkg.) active dry yeast

¼ cup warm water, heated to 110–120°

1 cup skim milk, *or* 1 cup buttermilk, heated to 110–120°

½ cup rolled, *or* quick, dry oats

2 Tbsp. peanut oil, *or* melted butter

2 Tbsp. honey

1 egg

¼ cup wheat germ

1 tsp. salt

2¾ cups whole wheat flour from hard wheat, also called bread flour, *divided*

3 Tbsp. wheat gluten

1. Grease a loaf pan that fits into your slow cooker, or a 1-lb. can that will stand upright in your cooker with the cooker lid on.

2. Put yeast, water, milk, oats, oil or butter, honey, egg, and wheat germ in good-sized mixing bowl. Mix together. Let stand until bubbly, about 10 minutes.

3. Stir in salt, about 2 cups flour, and gluten. When the mixture becomes too stiff to stir with a wooden spoon, use your hands to scrape and turn the dough until it forms a ball. If it remains too sticky, add a bit of the remaining flour.

4. When a ball forms, turn it onto a lightly floured countertop. Knead until smooth and elastic, about 5–8 minutes. Work in more of the remaining flour if you need it.

5. Turn dough immediately into the loaf pan or coffee can. Cover with greased aluminum foil. Let stand 5 minutes.

6. Place covered pan or can into the slow cooker on top of a trivet or metal jar rings. Cover the cooker. Bake on High 2½–3 hours. You'll know the bread is done when its sides brown and look crispy and its top is lightly brown and soft.

7. Remove pan from cooker. Let stand uncovered for 5 minutes. Then turn the pan or can upside down and take the bread out. Let it cool before slicing it.

Why I like this recipe —
This bread smells so absolutely tempting, you'll have a hard time not lifting the lid or pulling back the tin foil while it's cooking. But don't. This is great Saturday relaxation with a very satisfying pay-off.

Irish Soda Bread

Makes 8-10 servings
Prep. Time: 30 minutes ❦ Cooking Time: 2-3 hours
Ideal slow-cooker size: 5-quart

1 cup whole wheat flour

1 cup + 1 Tbsp. all-purpose flour, *divided*

½ tsp. salt

1 tsp. baking soda

¼ tsp. ground cardamom

1 egg

1 Tbsp. honey

★ 1 cup plain yogurt

★ TO MAKE YOUR OWN YOGURT, SEE PAGE 368.

TIP

This bread goes great with soups, but top it with jam or lemon curd for breakfast.

1. In a mixing bowl, stir together whole wheat flour, 1 cup all-purpose flour, salt, baking soda, and cardamom.

2. In a small bowl, beat the egg well. Add honey and yogurt to the egg and beat again.

3. Pour egg mixture into dry ingredients. Stir with a large spoon.

4. Clean the dough off the spoon and get ready to knead! Knead the dough for a few minutes, until it becomes satiny.

5. Place a large piece of parchment paper on the counter— it needs to be large enough so you can grab the corners and lift the bread out of the slow cooker when it's done.

6. Shape the dough into a round, low loaf. Set it in the middle of the parchment paper.

7. Use a sharp knife to make a large, shallow cross on the top of the loaf. Sprinkle the top of the loaf especially in the cross indentation with the remaining 1 Tbsp. flour.

8. Lift up the parchment paper, carrying the loaf in it like a sling, and place in slow cooker. Prop lid open at one end with a wooden spoon handle or chopstick.

9. Cook on High for 2-3 hours, until loaf is firm when tapped and tester comes out clean when inserted in the middle. Use the parchment paper to lift the finished loaf out of the cooker. Allow to cool 10 minutes or more before slicing. Best served warm, or toast it on day 2.

Why I like this recipe—
It's the perfect rustic bread
with a beautiful craggy
appearance—but because it's
a quick bread leavened with
baking soda, it's so easy and fast.

Why I like this recipe —

I love homemade bread, so I thought maybe the slow cooker could help me out with it. It does! I am not a proficient or confident bread-baker, but this method works for me and I hope you love it, too. Bread from the slow cooker tends to be heavy but moist, which is fine with me as I like hearty bread.

Oatmeal Bread

Makes 1 loaf

Prep. Time: 30 minutes ❦ *Cooking Time: 2½–3 hours*
Standing Time: 15–30 minutes ❦ *Rising Time: 1 hour*
Ideal slow-cooker size: 6-quart oval

½ cup dry
rolled oats

1 cup boiling water

1 Tbsp. (1 pkg.)
dry yeast

3 Tbsp. warm water

3 Tbsp. honey

1 tsp. salt

1 cup whole
wheat flour

1–2 cups unbleached
all-purpose flour

1. Place rolled oats in medium mixing bowl. Pour boiling water over oats. Stir. Allow to cool for 15–30 minutes or until room temperature.
2. Add yeast, warm water, honey, salt and whole wheat flour.
3. Whisk vigorously.
4. With wooden spoon or your hands, stir in 1 cup all-purpose flour. Start to knead, although the dough will be quite sticky. Gradually add up to another cup of all-purpose flour, kneading all the while.
5. When dough is smooth and firm, lift it up and pour a little oil underneath. Turn the ball of dough in the oil and use it to grease the bowl, turning dough ball so it's oiled completely.
6. Cover bowl with a damp kitchen towel and allow to rise until double, about 1 hour.
7. Press dough flat with hands or a rolling pin, and roll up into a loaf, tucking in ends securely. Place in greased 8×4 or 9×5 pan, whichever size will fit in your slow cooker. Or use a round baking dish.
8. Prick loaf all over with a fork to pop any air bubbles.
9. Place loaf pan or baking dish on a small trivet or metal jar lid or rings in slow cooker. Put lid on. Cook on High for 2½–3 hours, until loaf sounds hollow when tapped.
10. Remove loaf from pan or baking dish and allow to cool on rack before slicing—if you can wait that long!

Breakfasts and Brunches

Vegetable Omelet, page 290

Hearty Brunch Casserole

Makes 12-15 servings

Prep. Time: 30 minutes ❦ Cooking Time: 4 hours ❦ Chilling Time: 8 hours
Ideal slow-cooker size: 4-quart

8 slices firm white bread,
crusts removed

1 cup cubed ham *or* browned
sausage, drained, *divided*

2 spring onions, sliced, *divided*

½ cup sliced mushrooms, *divided*

½ cup diced bell pepper, *or*
broccoli florets, *divided*

1½ cups shredded extra-sharp
cheddar cheese, *divided*

½ cup freshly grated
Parmesan cheese, *divided*

5 eggs

1¾ cups whole milk

¼ tsp. dry mustard

½ tsp. seasoning salt

1 Tbsp. dried parsley

TOPPING:

1½ cups cornflakes

3 Tbsp. butter, melted

1. Grease the slow cooker crock. You are going to make layers. Cover bottom of crock with 4 slices of bread, cutting to fit. Slight overlap is okay (but don't omit any bread or that will alter the final texture!).

2. Top with half the meat, half the veggies, and half the cheeses.

3. Repeat layers once more, ending with cheese.

4. Whisk together eggs, milk, dry mustard, seasoning salt, and parsley. Mix well and pour over layers.

5. Cover and refrigerate for 8 hours, or overnight.

6. Remove from refrigerator 30 minutes before baking.

7. Place crock in cooker. Cook on Low for 3½ hours.

8. Combine cornflakes and butter and sprinkle over casserole. Drape several paper towels over the crock and then put the lid on. The paper towels will catch condensation and keep it off the cornflake topping. Cook an additional 30 minutes on Low.

Omelet Camping Casserole

Makes 10-12 servings
Prep. Time: 15 minutes ❧ *Cooking Time: 4-5 hours*
Ideal slow-cooker size: 5-quart

32-oz. bag frozen hash brown potatoes, *divided*

1 lb. cooked ham, cubed, *divided*

1 medium onion, diced, *divided*

1½ cups shredded cheddar cheese, *divided*

16 large eggs

1½ cups 2%, *or* whole milk

1 tsp. salt

1 tsp. pepper

1. Layer one-third each of frozen potatoes, ham, onions, and cheese in bottom of greased slow cooker. Repeat 2 times.

2. In a good-sized bowl, beat together eggs, milk, salt, and pepper. Pour over mixture in slow cooker.

3. Cover. Cook on Low 4-5 hours, until set in the middle and lightly brown around the edges.

Hearty French Toast

Makes 8 servings

Prep. Time: 20 minutes ❦ *Cooking Time: 2½–4 hours* ❦ *Chilling Time: 4 hours or overnight*
Ideal slow-cooker size: 5- or 6-quart

1 stick (½ cup) butter

1 cup brown sugar

2 tsp. molasses

8–10 slices whole wheat bread

3–5 Tbsp. peanut butter

6 eggs

1½ cups milk

1 tsp. cinnamon

¼ tsp. ground nutmeg

*Why I like this recipe —
I love any excuse to make
brunch, and this recipe is
a good one! I like to serve
this with fruit salad or
apple slices and a few
crisp pieces of bacon.*

1. In a saucepan, heat butter, brown sugar, and molasses together until sugar is dissolved and butter is melted. Stir occasionally to prevent sticking. When melted and blended together, pour into slow cooker.

2. Spread peanut butter on one side of each slice of bread, and then lay the bread on the syrup, peanut-butter side down. Cut the slices so they fit into the curve of the crock. If you need to stack some slices, that's fine.

3. In a mixing bowl, mix eggs, milk, cinnamon, and nutmeg together, and then pour on top of bread.

4. Cover and refrigerate for at least 4 hours, or overnight.

5. Place inner crock in electrical unit. Cook on Low for 3–4 hours, until set. If you need to hurry up the cooking time, turn the temperature to High after 1 hour and cook on High 1½ hours.

Creamy French Toast with Peaches

Makes 6 servings

Prep. Time: 20 minutes ❧ Cooking Time: 2–3 hours

Ideal slow-cooker size: 6-quart oval

10–12 slices, 1" thick, French *or* Italian bread

cream cheese, softened, at least 4 oz.

29-oz. can peach slices, drained

½ cup chopped pecans

3 eggs

¼ cup milk

⅓ cup maple syrup

2 Tbsp. butter, melted

1 tsp. cinnamon

1 tsp. vanilla

pinch salt

1. Spread cream cheese on both sides of bread slices.

2. Stack bread into greased crock. Prick each bread slice 3–4 times with a fork.

3. Top each layer of bread with peach slices and sprinkle chopped pecans over peaches, if desired.

4. In mixing bowl, beat eggs, and then combine with milk, maple syrup, butter, cinnamon, and vanilla. Whisk together.

5. Pour egg mixture over bread.

6. Cook on High for 2–3 hours, until egg mixture is set.

7. Serve with additional maple syrup, if you wish.

West Coast Eggs

Makes 10 servings
Prep. Time: 20 minutes   Cooking Time: 2-3 hours
Ideal slow-cooker size: 4-quart

10 eggs

2 cups cottage cheese

½ cup all-purpose flour

1 tsp. baking powder

½ tsp. salt

⅓ cup melted butter

1 lb. grated cheddar, *or* **Monterey Jack cheese**

1 *or* **2 4-oz. cans chopped green chilies,**
depending upon your taste preference

1. In a mixing bowl, beat together eggs, cottage cheese, flour, baking powder, salt, and butter.

2. Stir in cheese and green chilies.

3. Pour into greased slow cooker.

4. Cook on High for 2-3 hours, until set in the middle.

Vegetable Omelet

Makes 4-6 servings

Prep. Time: 20 minutes ❧ *Cooking Time: 2 hours*
Ideal slow-cooker size: 6-quart

5 eggs

⅓ cup milk

¼ tsp. salt

pinch black pepper

⅓ cup chopped onion

1 garlic clove, minced

1 cup small broccoli florets

1 cup thinly sliced zucchini

½ cup thinly sliced red bell pepper

½ cup your favorite grated cheese

1. Beat eggs with milk, salt, and pepper.
2. Add onion, garlic, broccoli, zucchini, and bell pepper. Stir.
3. Pour mixture into lightly greased baking dish that will fit in your slow cooker. Set dish on a small trivet or jar rings in slow cooker.
4. Cover and cook on High for 2 hours, until eggs are set and vegetables are softened.
5. Sprinkle with cheese and allow to melt before serving. Carefully, wearing oven mitts, remove hot dish from hot slow cooker. Slice and serve.

Huevos Rancheros

Makes 6 servings

Prep. Time: 20 minutes ❦ Cooking Time: 2½–3 hours
Ideal slow-cooker size: 5-quart

1 green bell pepper, chopped

1 small onion, chopped

14½-oz. can diced tomatoes, undrained

½ cup tomato sauce

½ tsp. salt

1 Tbsp. chili powder

½ tsp. ground cumin

pinch cinnamon

6 eggs

6 slices Monterey Jack cheese

6 flour tortillas

1. Place pepper, onion, diced tomatoes, tomato sauce, salt, chili powder, cumin, and cinnamon in slow cooker. Stir.

2. Cover and cook on High for 2 hours until vegetables soften.

3. With a wooden spoon, made 6 indentations in the sauce. Break an egg into each indentation.

4. Cover each with a slice of cheese.

5. Cover and cook on High for an additional 30–60 minutes, depending on how well done you like your eggs.

6. To serve, scoop a cheesy egg and some tomato mixture into a warmed tortilla. Have plenty of napkins on hand!

Easy Spinach Quiche

Makes 6 servings

Prep. Time: 20 minutes ❧ *Cooking Time: 3 hours* ❧ *Standing Time: 10 minutes*
Ideal slow-cooker size: 4- or 5-quart

2 pkgs. flat refrigerated
pie dough

5 eggs

1½ cups spinach dip (from
the refrigerated section
at the grocery store)

4 oz. prosciutto, chipped
ham, *or* Canadian bacon,
cut into small pieces

4 oz. pepper Jack
cheese, diced

1. Press pie crusts into cold slow cooker to create the
   crust. Overlap seams by ¼ inch, pressing to seal.
   Tear off pieces to fit up the sides, again pressing
   together at seams. Crimp the edges, if you wish.
2. Cover. Cook on High 1½ hours.
3. Beat eggs in a mixing bowl. Stir in spinach dip,
   prosciutto, and cheese. Pour into hot crust.
4. Cover. Cook on High 1½ hours or until filling is set.
5. Let stand 10 minutes before serving.

Meatless Breakfast Bake

Makes 8-10 servings
Prep. Time: 15 minutes   Cooking Time: 3-4 hours
Ideal slow-cooker size: 4- or 5-quart

TIP

To obtain stale bread, allow bread to sit out, uncovered, overnight. Alternatively, toast it lightly in a toaster or oven and allow to cool.

4 cups cubed stale bread

½ cup sliced mushrooms

¼ cup chopped onion

2 cups shredded sharp cheddar cheese

10 eggs, slightly beaten

4 cups milk

1 tsp. salt

freshly ground pepper, to taste

1 tsp. dry mustard

1 large tomato, sliced

1. Place bread in buttered crock. Sprinkle with mushrooms, onions, and cheese.

2. Combine eggs, milk, salt, pepper, and mustard. Pour evenly over the layers in crock.

3. Lay the tomato slices on top. Cover and cook for 3–4 hours on Low.

Why I like this recipe —
    Eggs, cheese, and vegetables are plenty tasty even without meat. Make this in summer when the tomatoes are at their beautiful best and you don't want to heat up the house with the oven.

Baked Oatmeal

Makes 4-6 servings
Prep. Time: 10 minutes ❦ Cooking Time: 3-4 hours
Ideal slow-cooker size: 2- or 3-quart

½ cup oil

¾ cup brown sugar

1 tsp. salt

2 eggs

1½ cups milk

3 cups uncooked
oatmeal, rolled
or quick

2 tsp. baking powder

1. Combine oil, brown sugar, salt, eggs, and milk in blender. Whip until well-blended.

2. Combine with dry oatmeal and baking powder in mixing bowl. Mix well.

3. Pour into greased slow cooker.

4. Cook on Low for 3-4 hours, until set in the middle and browned around the edges.

5. Serve hot with fruit and milk poured over, or if you have time, allow it to stand in the cooling slow cooker up to an hour for easier cutting and serving.

Variations —

- *Swap out a ¼ cup of the oil and replace with applesauce or plain yogurt.*

- *Add 1 tsp. cinnamon, 1 cup chopped apples, and ¼ cup chopped nuts for a version that tastes a bit like apple crisp.*

- *Sprinkle the top with ½ cup of frozen raspberries or blueberries before cooking. Serve with dollops of vanilla yogurt.*

- *Add 1 cup raisins and 1 tsp. cinnamon for an oatmeal-cookie vibe. You see there's a lot of room for variations, right? Use the spices and fruits you enjoy to make this recipe your own!*

Steel Cut Oatmeal — 3 Versions

QUICK
and
EASY

Makes 6-8 servings
Prep. Time: 5-10 minutes ❦ Cooking Time: 6-8 hours
Ideal slow-cooker size: 4-quart

2 cups steel cut oats (do **not** substitute old-fashioned or quick-cooking oats)

3 cups water

1 cup apple cider

4 cups milk, plus more for serving

1 tsp. salt

2 Tbsp. butter

1 good-sized apple, chopped

2–4 Tbsp. brown sugar

1 tsp. ground cinnamon

¾–1 cup chopped walnuts

1. Place all ingredients into a 4-quart slow cooker except for walnuts. (If you want to make a smaller amount, use a smaller slow cooker).

2. Cover and cook on Low 6-8 hours, or overnight. If the oatmeal gets brown and crispy around the edges, just stir it down into the oatmeal. It adds flavor.

3. Serve with milk. Top each serving with 2 Tbsp. chopped walnuts.

Variation #1—

- *Replace apple cider with orange juice.*

- *Instead of 1 chopped apple, use 1 cup dried cranberries.*

- *Drop the cinnamon. Stir in ¼ tsp. cardamom.*

- *Top with sliced almonds instead of chopped walnuts.*

Variation #2—

- *Follow the original recipe. But swap 1 cup blueberries (fresh or frozen) for the apple. Keep everything else the same.*

- *Or follow Variation 1, and substitute 1 cup chopped dried apricots or dates, or go with 1 cup raisins instead of the dried cranberries. Use either cider or orange juice.*

Cheese Grits

Makes 6-8 servings
Prep. Time: 25 minutes ❧ *Cooking Time: 2-2¼ hours*
Ideal slow-cooker size: 3- or 4-quart

4 cups water

1½ tsp. salt

1 cup uncooked grits

3 Tbsp. butter

minced garlic to taste, *optional*

1¼ cups grated sharp cheddar cheese, *or* Monterey Jack/cheddar combined

2 eggs, room temperature

1. Place water in large saucepan, add salt, and cover. Bring to boil.

2. Add grits and stir for 1 minute.

3. Cover and cook until thick and creamy, about 5-7 minutes. Stir occasionally.

4. Add butter, optional garlic, and cheese to pan. Stir.

5. Beat eggs in a small bowl. Stir in ¼ cup cooked grits to temper the eggs so they don't scramble and blend together. Add egg mixture back to saucepan of grits. Stir.

6. Pour grits mixture into lightly greased slow cooker. Cover. Cook on High 2 hours or until set. If watery around the edges, remove lid and cook uncovered for 20 minutes.

Grain and Fruit Hot Cereal

QUICK
and
EASY

Makes 10-12 servings
Prep. Time: 15 minutes ❦ *Cooking Time: 6-7 hours*
Ideal slow-cooker size: 5-quart

¾ cup dehulled barley, also called pot or scotch barley, *or* pearl barley

¾ cup steel-cut oats

¾ cup quinoa *or* millet

¾ cup wheat berries

¾ cup dried blueberries

¾ cup dried cranberries

4½ cups water

4 cups apple cider *or* apple juice

2" cinnamon stick

½ tsp. salt

honey, for serving

milk, for serving

1. Combine grains, dried fruit, water, apple cider, cinnamon stick, and salt in slow cooker.

2. Cover and cook on Low for 6-7 hours, until grains are soft and liquid is absorbed.

3. Serve hot with milk and honey as desired.

TIP
You can use raisins in place of the dried cranberries and blueberries. Other whole grains such as rye or spelt can be used instead of the wheat berries.

Why I like this recipe—
This is a simple, healthy breakfast. The plump fruit and touch of cinnamon make it special. If you have a programmable slow-cooker, start the cereal at bedtime and when it's finished cooking, the cooker can hold it at warm until breakfast. It's luxurious to wake up to hot breakfast! Otherwise, just cook the cereal in the daytime and reheat it in the microwave with a bit of milk to loosen it up for a quick, satisfying breakfast.

Why I like this recipe—

My daughter introduced me to this granola, and I love the flavors. I, in turn, introduced her to the concept of making granola in the slow cooker! It's great for keeping a cool kitchen in the summer, and I am much less likely to burn the granola using this method.

Granola

Makes 8 cups
Prep. Time: 10 minutes ❦ Cooking Time: 2-3 hours
Ideal slow-cooker size: 5- or 6-quart

3 cups uncooked quick oats

3 cups uncooked rolled oats

½ cup oat bran

¾ cup slivered almonds

½ cup sunflower seeds

2 Tbsp. heavy whipping cream

⅔ cup honey

⅓ cup vegetable oil

1 tsp. vanilla

1 tsp. cinnamon

½ tsp. salt

1. Mix all ingredients in a large bowl—clean hands work well for this.

2. Place in lightly greased slow cooker. You want the lid to be vented; either prop up the lid with a chopstick or wooden spoon handle, or if you have an oval cooker, turn the lid sideways.

3. Cook for an hour on High, stirring every 20 minutes or so (set a timer so you don't forget!). Then switch the cooker to Low and continue to cook for another 1-2 hours, still stirring. The Granola will get tan and dried looking when it is done, and it will crisp up even more as it cools.

4. When Granola is done, pour it onto parchment paper or a large baking sheet to cool completely. If you like clumps in your granola, allow it to cool undisturbed; otherwise, use a spoon to break up the chunks.

5. When thoroughly cool, store in airtight container for up to 10 days or freeze for longer storage. Serve as breakfast cereal with milk and dried cranberries.

Appetizers, Snacks, and Beverages

Salmon-Stuffed Mushrooms, page 305

Why I like this recipe —
These make a party special. There's some chopping going on here.
But it's not hard. Just start early enough.
The people who eat these will think you're
an amazing cook. Take the credit.

Salmon-Stuffed Mushrooms

Makes 20 mushrooms

Prep. Time: 30–40 minutes ❦ *Cooking Time: 2 hours 10 minutes*
Ideal slow-cooker size: 6-quart

20 large, fresh, button mushrooms

1 Tbsp. extra-virgin olive oil, *or* hazelnut oil

¼ cup chopped red onions

2 Tbsp. chopped hazelnuts, walnuts, *or* pecans

¼ tsp. chopped fresh dill

½ tsp. Worcestershire sauce

¼ tsp. salt

4-oz. smoked, *or* steamed, salmon, flaked

salmon roe, *optional*

minced, fresh, flat-leaf parsley, *optional*

1. Clean mushrooms and remove stems. Place mushrooms stem-side up in the bottom of the slow cooker crock.

2. Cover. Cook on Low 2 hours, or until mushrooms are just tender.

3. Half an hour before the end of the mushrooms' cooking time, stir together the oil and onions in a microwave-safe bowl. Cover. Microwave on High for 1 minute. Stir. Repeat if you'd like the onions to be a bit softer.

4. Stir the nuts, dill, Worcestershire sauce, and salt into the onions. Stir in the salmon. Let stand for 20 minutes.

5. Take the mushrooms out of the cooker. Turn them upside down on paper towels to drain.

6. When the mushroom caps are cool enough to hold, fill them with the salmon mixture. Return them to the cooker, filled side up.

7. Cover. Cook on High for 10–15 minutes, or until the salmon mixture is bubbly.

8. If you want, sprinkle the cooked mushrooms with salmon roe and minced parsley just before serving.

Easy Bacon Squares

Makes 12–15 servings

Prep. Time: 20 minutes if you're not cooking the bacon ❦ *Cooking Time: 2–3 hours*
Ideal slow-cooker size: 4-quart

8-oz. pkg. refrigerated crescent roll dough

8–10 slices bacon, fried, drained, crumbled, about ⅔ cup total

12-oz. shredded Swiss cheese

3 eggs, beaten

¾ cup milk

1 Tbsp. minced chives, *or* any herb you wish

½ tsp. salt

1. Grease the insides of the inner crock. Cut the dough into 3 or 4 pieces so you can work more easily. Then press the dough evenly over the bottom and up the sides an inch or two, depending on the size of your cooker. Overlap the seams where 2 pieces meet and press down on the seams to keep them from separating.

2. In a good-sized bowl, combine the remaining ingredients and pour over the dough.

3. Cook for 2–3 hours on Low. The crust should be browning but not burning, and the eggs should be set but not dry.

4. Let stand for 10 minutes. Then cut into wedges or squares and serve.

Hot Wings Dip

TIP

If you have any leftover dip, it makes a fantastic sandwich the next day with sliced tomato and lettuce.

Makes 16 4oz servings   *Makes 8 cups*
Prep. Time: 15 minutes   *Cooking Time: 1-2 hours*
Ideal slow-cooker size: 3-quart

2 8-oz. pkgs. cream cheese, at room temperature

8 oz. Ranch dressing

12-oz. bottle hot wing sauce, *or* less if that's too spicy for you

3 cups cubed, grilled chicken

2 cups grated extra-sharp cheddar cheese

1. Combine cream cheese, Ranch dressing, and hot wing sauce. Mix well.

2. Add chicken and cheddar cheese. Pour into greased slow cooker.

3. Cook on High for 1-2 hours.

4. Serve warm with tortilla chips or baguette slices and celery.

Rio Bean Dip

Makes 12-16 servings ❧ *Makes 6 cups*
Prep. Time: 20 minutes ❧ Cooking Time: 3 hours
Ideal slow-cooker size: 3-quart

½ lb. bulk sausage

½ lb. hot sausage, squeezed out of casing

⅔ cup chopped onions

2 16-oz. cans of your favorite baked beans

1 cup barbecue sauce

1. Brown both kinds of sausage and onions in skillet. Drain off drippings. Place in blender or food processor.
2. Add rest of ingredients to food processor or blender with sausage and onions. Blend until smooth.
3. Pour into slow cooker. Heat on Low for 3 hours.
4. Serve warm with cheese crackers or tortilla chips.

Zesty Bean Dip

Makes 10-12 servings

Prep. Time: 20 minutes ❧ *Cooking Time: 1-4 hours*

Ideal slow-cooker size: 2-quart

15½-oz. can black beans, rinsed and drained

1 tsp. ground cumin

½ tsp. salt

2 Tbsp. butter, at room temperature

2 spring onions, diced

8 oz. pkg. cream cheese, at room temperature

12-oz. jar salsa, in whatever heat or flavor you prefer, *divided*

¼ cup chopped cilantro

1. Pour beans into slow cooker. Add cumin, salt, and butter.

2. With a potato masher, mash together until mostly uniform and mixed. Pat the bean mixture over the bottom of the slow cooker.

3. Sprinkle with onions.

4. In a bowl, beat the cream cheese. Add ⅔ cup of the salsa and beat again.

5. Dollop the cream cheese mixture evenly over the onions. Spread gently to cover.

6. Cover and cook on Low for 3-4 hours, or High for 1-2 hours, until heated and bubbly.

7. Spread remaining salsa over the hot dip and sprinkle with cilantro. Serve as a dip with tortilla chips.

*Why I like this recipe —
It's tasty! I like to serve this to my
football-loving family when a game is on.*

Rosemary Walnuts

Makes 8 servings ❦ *Makes 2 cups*
Prep. Time: 5 minutes ❦ *Cooking Time: 1-2 hours*
Ideal slow-cooker size: 4-quart

half stick (¼ cup)
butter, melted

1 lb. walnut halves

4 Tbsp. finely chopped
fresh rosemary, *or*
4 tsp. dried rosemary

½ tsp. salt, *optional*

1 tsp. paprika

1. Mix together butter and walnuts in slow cooker until nuts are well coated.

2. Stir in rosemary, salt if you wish, and paprika.

3. Cover. Cook on High for 15 minutes. Stir.

4. Then reduce heat to Low and cook **uncovered** at least 45 minutes longer, and up to 1½ more hours.

5. Serve warm. Or spread them out on a baking sheet to cool before storing. They'll crisp even more as they cool.

Autumn Latte

Makes 6 servings
Prep. Time: 5 minutes   Cooking Time: 2 hours
Ideal slow-cooker size: 3-quart

4 cups 2% milk

1½ cups strong brewed coffee, decaf *or* regular

½ cup cooked, puréed pumpkin (from a can is fine)

2 Tbsp. sugar

2–4 Tbsp. dark brown sugar, depending how sweet you like your latte

1 Tbsp. vanilla extract

½ tsp. cinnamon, plus more for garnish

¼ tsp. ground cloves

¼ tsp. ground nutmeg

⅛ tsp. ground ginger

pinch salt

whipped cream, for garnish

1. Combine milk, coffee, pumpkin, sugars, vanilla, cinnamon, cloves, nutmeg, ginger, and salt in slow cooker. Whisk until pumpkin is mixed in well.

2. Cover and cook on High for 2 hours until steaming hot. Whisk again.

3. Ladle into mugs. Dollop whipped cream on top and sprinkle with cinnamon to be fancy.

TIP

I saw one of my friends whiz her latte into a milky froth with an inexpensive little frother instead of putting whipped cream on top – that was fun!

Mulled Cider Served Hot

Makes 8 servings

Prep. Time: 5 minutes   Cooking Time: 5 hours
Ideal slow-cooker size: 3½-quart

**2 qts. (half-gallon)
apple cider**

**2–4 Tbsp. brown sugar,
depending on how sweet
you like your cider**

½ tsp. vanilla

1 cinnamon stick

4 cloves

1. Combine all ingredients in a slow cooker.

2. Cover. Cook on Low 5 hours to blend the flavors (and make the house smell good!). Stir before serving.

3. You can keep this on Warm for hours if you're hosting a party. But fish out the cinnamon stick and cloves after the Cider has heated for 5 hours so those spices don't begin to dominate the flavor.

Hot Buttered Lemonade

QUICK *and* EASY

Makes 5-6 servings ***Makes 6 cups***
Prep. Time: 10–15 minutes *Cooking Time: 2½ hours*
Ideal slow-cooker size: 2-quart

4½ cups water
¾ cup sugar
1½ tsp. grated lemon zest
¾ cup fresh lemon juice
2 Tbsp. butter
5–6 cinnamon sticks

1. Combine water, sugar, lemon zest, lemon juice, and butter in slow cooker.
2. Cover. Cook on High for 2½ hours, or until hot the whole way through.
3. Serve very hot with a cinnamon stick in each mug.

Why I like this recipe—
This drink has great punch.
And it takes well to variations.

Sweets and Desserts

Fudgy Chocolate Cake, page 316

Fudgy Chocolate Cake

Makes 8-12 servings

Prep. Time: 20 minutes 🌣 Cooking Time: 1-2 hours 🌣 Standing Time: 25 minutes

Ideal slow-cooker size: 4-quart

1 cup all-purpose flour

2 tsp. baking powder

2 Tbsp. butter

2 oz. semisweet chocolate, *or* ⅓ cup chocolate chips

1 cup brown sugar, *divided*

3 Tbsp. plus ⅓ cup Dutch-processed cocoa, *divided*

1 Tbsp. vanilla extract

¼ tsp. salt

⅓ cup skim milk

1 egg yolk

1½ cups hot water

1. Coat inside of slow cooker with cooking spray.
2. In mixing bowl, whisk together flour and baking powder. Set aside.
3. In a large microwave-safe mixing bowl, melt the butter and chocolate in the microwave. Mix well.
4. Whisk in ⅔ cup brown sugar, 3 Tbsp. cocoa powder, vanilla, salt, milk, and egg yolk.
5. Add the flour mixture. Stir until thoroughly mixed.
6. Pour batter into slow cooker. Spread evenly.
7. Whisk together remaining ⅓ cup brown sugar, ⅓ cup cocoa powder, and 1½ cups hot water until sugar is dissolved. Pour over batter in slow cooker. Do **not** stir.
8. Cover. Cook on High 1-2 hours. The cake will be very moist and floating on a layer of molten chocolate when it's done. And you'll know it is done cooking when nearly all the cake is set and its edges begin to pull away from the sides of the pot.
9. Turn off slow cooker and remove lid. Try not to let the condensed steam from the lid drip onto the cake.
10. Let cool for 25 minutes before cutting and spooning onto individual plates.

TIP
Make sure you dig deep when you serve so everyone gets a spoonful of this fudgy sauce.

Why I like this recipe —
I absolutely love the puddles of
chocolate that this cake sits on.

Chocolate Peanut Butter Cake

Makes 8 servings

Prep. Time: 15 minutes   Cooking Time: 1½–2 hours

Ideal slow-cooker size: 2- or 3-quart

1½ cups sugar, *divided*

1 cup all-purpose flour

1½ tsp. baking powder

⅔ cup milk

½ cup peanut butter

2 Tbsp. oil

1 tsp. vanilla

5 Tbsp. unsweetened cocoa powder

2 cups boiling water

1. Butter or spray interior of slow cooker.

2. Mix ½ cup sugar, flour, and baking powder together in a small bowl.

3. In another larger bowl, mix milk, peanut butter, oil, and vanilla together. Beat well.

4. Stir dry ingredients into milk-peanut butter mixture just until combined. Spread in buttered slow-cooker.

5. In bowl, combine cocoa powder and remaining 1 cup sugar. Add water, stirring until well mixed. Pour slowly into slow cooker. Do **not** stir.

6. Cover. Cook on High 1½–2 hours, or until toothpick inserted in center of cake comes out clean.

7. Serve warm with vanilla ice cream.

Oatmeal Tandy Cake

Makes 12 servings
Prep. Time: 25 minutes   Cooking Time: 3 hours
Ideal slow-cooker size: 5- or 6-quart

1½ cups boiling water

1 cup dry quick oats

½ cup sugar

1 cup light brown sugar

½ cup shortening

2 eggs

1½ cups all-purpose flour

1 tsp. baking soda

½ tsp. salt

1 tsp. cinnamon

6-oz. package chocolate peanut butter cups

1. Pour boiling water over quick oats in a small bowl. Let stand a few minutes.

2. In a separate bowl, cream together sugars, shortening, and eggs. Add oatmeal mixture.

3. In a small bowl, combine flour, baking soda, salt, and cinnamon. Add to egg/oatmeal mixture.

4. Pour into a greased and floured slow cooker.

5. Chop peanut butter cups coarsely. Sprinkle over batter.

6. Put 2 paper towels over the top of the crock before you put the lid on. The paper towels will absorb the condensation and prevent it from dripping down on the cake.

7. Covered, with the paper towels in place, cook on High for 3 hours or until tester inserted in middle comes out clean.

8. Remove crock from electrical unit and let it sit with the cake, uncovered, until nearly cool. Slice with a plastic or silicone knife and serve.

Why I like this recipe —
I love the juxtaposition of spice with the chocolate peanut butter cups. Of course, the oatmeal does not make this a healthy cake, just a fun alternative to the classic oatmeal cake with the broiled topping.

Why I like this recipe—

Bread puddings always surprise me with their delicious texture and flavor. How can bread be transformed so beautifully? Here, the coffee and almonds are a pleasing addition to the chocolate flavor.

Mocha Bread Pudding

Makes 12-15 servings

Prep. Time: 20 minutes ❦ Cooking Time: 2-3 hours ❦ Standing Time: 30 minutes
Ideal slow-cooker size: 6-quart

1 Tbsp. butter

12 cups cubed hearty white bread, *or* very light whole wheat, preferably day-old

4 cups whole milk

6 eggs

1 Tbsp. vanilla

⅓ cup sugar

¾ cup brown sugar

¼ cup unsweetened cocoa powder

1½ Tbsp. instant coffee granules

¾ cup semi-sweet chocolate chips

½ cup sliced almonds, toasted

1. Grease inner crock with butter.

2. Place bread cubes in buttered slow cooker.

3. In a mixing bowl, beat together milk, eggs, and vanilla.

4. Add sugar, brown sugar, cocoa powder, and coffee. Stir well.

5. Pour milk mixture over bread cubes. Stir and gently press to get all the bread cubes into the milk mixture.

6. Sprinkle with chocolate chips.

7. Cover and cook on High for 2-3 hours, until puffy and until liquid is gone from the middle. Sprinkle with almonds and press them gently into the surface of the bread pudding.

8. Allow to sit with the lid off for at least 30 minutes, to firm up and cool down a bit. Serve warm with ice cream or caramel sauce or both!

Cook's Tip —

If you bought fresh bread just for this recipe (I do), take it out of its wrapper and allow the slices to sit in the air for a few hours and even overnight. Somehow stale bread gives a better texture to a bread pudding, even though you're going to moisten it up with milk and eggs.

Pumpkin Chocolate Chip Cake

Makes 6-8 servings

Prep. Time: 30 minutes ❦ Cooking Time: 2-3 hours ❦ Standing Time: 10-30 minutes

Ideal slow-cooker size: 4-quart

1¾ cups sugar

4 eggs

2 cups cooked pumpkin, canned *or* your own fresh

1 cup vegetable oil

2 cups all-purpose flour

½ cup whole wheat flour

2 tsp. baking powder

1 tsp. baking soda

½ tsp. salt

1½ tsp. ground cinnamon

½ tsp. ground cloves

½ tsp. ground nutmeg

¼ tsp. ground allspice

¼ tsp. ground ginger

1 cup chocolate chips

1 cup chopped walnuts

1. In a mixing bowl, combine sugar and eggs. Beat well. Add pumpkin and oil and mix well.
2. Separately, stir together flours, baking powder, baking soda, salt and spices.
3. Add chocolate chips and walnuts on top of wet ingredients. Add flour mixture on top.
4. Gently stir together until just mixed.
5. Pour into greased slow cooker. Cover and cook on High for 2-3 hours, until tester inserted in middle comes out clean.
6. Remove crock from electrical unit. Uncover. Allow cake to sit for 10-30 minutes before slicing with a silicone (or other non-scratching) knife. Once you wiggle the first piece out with a spatula, the rest will come out more easily.

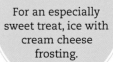

TIP

For an especially sweet treat, ice with cream cheese frosting.

Apple Cake

Makes 8 servings
Prep. Time: 20 minutes ❦ *Cooking Time: 1-1½ hours* ❦ *Standing Time: 15-20 minutes*
Ideal slow-cooker size: 6-quart

half stick (¼ cup) butter, melted

1 cup sugar

1 egg, beaten

1 cup all-purpose flour

½ tsp. baking soda

½ tsp. baking powder

½ tsp. cinnamon

¼ tsp. salt

2 cups chopped apples, peeled or not

½ cup chopped walnuts

1 tsp. vanilla

1. Cream butter, sugar, and egg together in a good-sized bowl.

2. Mix all the dry ingredients together in a separate bowl. Stir into sugar mixture until fully combined.

3. Fold in the apples, walnuts, and vanilla.

4. Spread the batter into a greased and floured bread pan or baking dish that fits into your slow cooker. Cover the baking dish with aluminum foil. Set into the slow cooker on metal jar rings or a trivet.

5. Cover with the slow cooker lid. Bake on High 2-3 hours. Poke a toothpick into the center of the cake after it's been baking 2 hours. If the toothpick comes out clean, the cake is done. If it doesn't, cover and continue cooking for 15-30 minutes.

6. When the cake is finished, carefully lift the hot pan out of the hot cooker, set it on a wire rack, and let it cool for 15-20 minutes before cutting and serving.

Why I like this recipe—

I panicked when I first made this cake. I was sure I should have used more flour, sugar, and eggs. But I got myself stopped before I started dumping things in. I decided to see if the apples were juicy enough to hold things together and wind up with a dense and delicious finish. And it worked!! Look at this recipe. You've got everything you need in the house to make it any time.

Shoofly Loaf

Makes 16–20 servings

Prep. Time: 20 minutes ❧ *Cooking Time: 3½–4 hours* ❧ *Standing Time: 2 hours*
Ideal slow-cooker size: 6-quart oval

1 cup whole wheat flour

1 cup all-purpose flour

1 cup brown sugar

½ cup (1 stick) cup butter, softened

1 cup boiling water

¼ cup unsulphured blackstrap molasses

¼ cup mild baking molasses

1 tsp. baking soda

¼ tsp. ground cinnamon

¼ tsp. salt

TIP

Good go-alongs are vanilla ice cream, of course, or applesauce, but also a fresh fruit salad or a few slices of a beautiful peach.

1. Combine both flours, brown sugar, and butter until crumbly. Measure out and set aside ¾ cup crumbs for topping.

2. Combine boiling water, two kinds of molasses, and baking soda in a heatproof bowl.

3. Pour water mixture into remaining crumbs. Add cinnamon and salt. Mix well to make batter.

4. Pour batter into well-greased 9 × 5 loaf pan. Sprinkle with reserved ¾ cup crumbs.

5. Place a small trivet or metal jar rings in slow cooker. Set loaf pan on it. Vent slow cooker lid at one end with a chopstick or wooden spoon handle.

6. Cook on High for 3½–4 hours, until tester inserted in middle comes out clean.

7. Carefully remove pan from slow cooker. Allow loaf to cool in the pan for 2 hours. Either slice in the pan and lift out slices individually, or slide a knife around the edges of the loaf to lift it out completely. Be careful not to flip it upside down in the process and lose the crumbs!

Why I like this recipe —

It's kind of a Pennsylvania Dutch thing to have shoofly pie on the breakfast table, but this recipe is a much easier option than making a pie crust, I think. I serve slices of this with breakfast or as a family dessert during the week.

QUICK
and
EASY

Quick Apple Cobbler

Makes 8 servings
Prep. Time: 10 minutes ❧ Cooking Time: 1½–2 hours
Ideal slow-cooker size: 4-quart

1 stick (½ cup) butter	1. Grease the inside of your slow cooker well.
1 cup sugar	2. Melt the butter. Pour into the slow cooker.
1 cup all-purpose flour	3. Mix the sugar, flour, baking powder, salt, and cinnamon together.
2 tsp. baking powder	
½ tsp. salt	4. Stir in milk until smooth. Spoon into the cooker on top of the butter. Do **not** stir.
½ tsp. cinnamon	
1 cup milk	5. Spoon the chopped apples over the batter. Again, **don't** stir.
4 cups chopped apples, peeled *or* not	6. Cover. Cook on High 1½–2 hours, or until a toothpick stuck into the center of the cake comes out clean.
	7. Serve warm with milk or ice cream.

Plum Cobbler

Makes 9 servings

Prep. Time: 10-15 minutes ❦ Cooking Time: 1½-1¾ hours

Ideal slow-cooker size: 4-quart

¼ cup (half stick) butter, softened

¼ cup sugar

2 eggs

1 tsp. grated lemon peel

1 cup all-purpose flour

1 tsp. baking powder

¼ cup milk

2½ cups sliced fresh plums, unpeeled (about 4 medium-sized ones)

2 tsp. cinnamon

½ cup brown sugar

1. In a mixing bowl, cream butter and sugar together.
2. Beat in the eggs and lemon peel.
3. In a separate bowl, combine the flour and baking powder.
4. Stir the flour mixture into the creamed ingredients. Add the milk, mixing well.
5. Pour batter into lightly greased slow cooker.
6. Arrange plums on top of batter.
7. In a small bowl, stir together the cinnamon and brown sugar. Sprinkle over the plums.
8. Cover and cook on High for 1-1¼ hours, until cobbler is nearly set in the middle and plums are juicy. Remove lid and cook another 30 minutes on High.

Date Loaf Cake

Makes 15 servings

Prep. Time: 20 minutes ❦ *Cooking Time: 4 hours* ❦ *Standing Time: 30 minutes*
Ideal slow-cooker size: 6-quart

1 tsp. baking soda

1 cup chopped, pitted dates

1 cup boiling water

2 Tbsp. butter, at room temperature

1 egg

1 cup sugar

1½ cups all-purpose flour

1 tsp. vanilla

pinch nutmeg

1 cup chopped walnuts

caramel sauce, *optional*

whipped cream, *optional*

1. In a small bowl, sprinkle baking soda over dates. Add boiling water. Let stand, cooling, at least 30 minutes.
2. In a mixing bowl, cream butter, egg, and sugar. Add cooled date mixture.
3. Beat in flour, vanilla, and nutmeg. Stir in walnuts.
4. Pour into greased loaf pan that will fit in your slow cooker.
5. Place pan on small trivet or metal jar rings in slow cooker. Prop slow cooker lid open at one end with a chopstick or wooden spoon handle.
6. Cook on High for 4 hours or until tester inserted in middle of loaf comes out clean.
7. Wear oven mitts to lift hot cake out of hot slow cooker. Turn the cake out onto a rack to cool.
8. To serve, pour a little puddle of caramel sauce on a plate. Add a slice of date cake next to it with a dollop of whipped cream on top.

TIP

If you're lucky enough to get your hands on black walnuts, they add a wonderful flavor dimension.

Why I like this recipe —
This is an old-fashioned dessert which I love. Serve it in plain slices for an easy picnic dessert, or dress it up with the sauce and whipped cream as described to delight guests.

Orange Poppy Seed Cake

Makes 10-12 servings
Prep. Time: 20-30 minutes ⚘ Cooking Time: 2-3 hours
Ideal slow-cooker size: 3-quart

1 stick (½ cup) butter, softened to room temperature

¾ cup sugar

2 large eggs

½ cup sour cream

⅓ cup poppy seeds

¼ cup orange juice

1 Tbsp. grated orange rind

1 tsp. vanilla

1¼ cups all-purpose flour

½ tsp. baking powder

¼ tsp. baking soda

pinch of salt

confectioners sugar

1. In a mixing bowl cream together butter and sugar until the mixture is light and fluffy.

2. Beat in the eggs, one at a time. Beat in sour cream, poppy seeds, orange juice, orange rind, and vanilla.

3. Sift together the flour, baking powder, baking soda, and salt. Add to the batter and mix well.

4. Pour into your greased slow cooker. Cover. Cook on High 2-3 hours, or until a toothpick inserted into the center of the cake comes out clean.

5. Let the cake cool completely before taking it out of the slow cooker. Dust it with confectioners sugar before serving. I do this by putting confectioners sugar in a small mesh strainer and tapping it lightly so the sugar sifts down.

Pumpkin Pie Pudding with Streusel Topping

Makes 4 servings
Prep. Time: 15 minutes ❧ Cooking Time: 3 hours
Ideal slow-cooker size: 3-quart

PUDDING:

15-oz. can, *or* 2 cups, mashed pumpkin

14-oz. can sweetened condensed milk

2 eggs, beaten

1 tsp. ground cinnamon

½ tsp. ground ginger

½ tsp. ground nutmeg

½ tsp. salt

STREUSEL:

½ cup light brown sugar

½ cup all-purpose flour

half stick (4 Tbsp.) cold butter

¼ cup chopped nuts (I like walnuts *or* pecans)

1. Grease the interior of your slow cooker crock. Add all pudding ingredients and mix well until the lumps are gone.
2. Cover. Cook on Low 2½ hours.
3. While the pudding is cooking, mix the brown sugar and flour together in a medium-sized bowl. Cut the butter into chunks and add to the dry ingredients.
4. Using a pastry cutter, or two knives, cut the butter into the sugar and flour until the mixture gets crumbly. Stir in the nuts.
5. When the pudding finishes cooking, crumble streusel over top. Turn the cooker to High. Do not cover. Cook for 30 minutes.
6. Let the pudding cool before serving.

Pumpkin Pecan Pie

Makes 8-10 servings
Prep. Time: 20-30 minutes ❦ Cooking Time: 1½ hours
Ideal slow-cooker size: 4- or 5-quart

2 pkgs. flat refrigerated pie dough

4 eggs

16-oz. can pumpkin

¾ cup sugar

½ cup dark corn syrup

1 tsp. cinnamon

¼ tsp. salt

1 cup pecans

TIP

You can make this pie, no matter the shape of your slow cooker.

1. Press the pie crusts into your cold slow cooker. Overlap the seams by ¼ inch, pressing to seal them. Tear off pieces so that the crusts fit partway up the sides, pressing the pieces together at all seams.

2. In a large bowl beat the eggs lightly. Then stir in the pumpkin, sugar, corn syrup, cinnamon, and salt, and mix well.

3. Pour into the unbaked pie shell. Arrange the pecans on top.

4. Cover. Cook on High for 1½ hours, or until the filling is set and a knife blade inserted in the center comes out clean.

Why I like this recipe —
It's always fun to see what a slow cooker can do. Remember that a slow cooker doesn't heat up your kitchen, or it can substitute if your oven is full. Don't forget—it works for you.

Easy Baked Apples

Makes 12 servings
Prep. Time: 30 minutes ❧ Cooking Time: 2–4 hours
Ideal slow-cooker size: 6-quart

12 small, crisp apples

½ cup raisins

½ cup chopped nuts—walnuts *or* pecans work well

1 cup brown sugar

½ tsp. nutmeg

1 tsp. cinnamon

3 slices fresh lemon

2 tsp. lemon juice

1¼ cups boiling water

1. Wash the apples and core them while keeping them whole. Starting at the stem, peel each one about halfway down.

2. In a small bowl, stir the raisins and chopped nuts together. Spoon some of the mixture into each apple, dividing the raisins and nuts evenly among the apples.

3. Stack the stuffed apples into the slow cooker, but not squarely on top of each other. Do your best to have them sit upright.

4. Combine the sugar, nutmeg, and cinnamon in a small saucepan. Add the lemon slices and lemon juice and pour boiling water over everything. Boil the ingredients together for about 5 minutes. Pour the syrup over the apples in the slow cooker.

5. Cover. Cook on Low 2–4 hours, or until the apples are as tender as you like them. Spoon the sauce over them again before serving. Serve hot, room temperature, or cold.

Rustic Apple Squares

Makes 12 servings
Prep. Time: 25 minutes   Cooking Time: 4 hours
Ideal slow-cooker size: 6-quart oval

2 cups all-purpose flour

3 tsp. baking powder

½ tsp. salt

½ cup (1 stick) cold butter

6 Tbsp. milk

6 cups sliced firm apples, peeled

1 tsp. cinnamon

pinch nutmeg

½–1 cup sugar, depending on how sweet your apples are

1 cup boiling water

1. In a large mixing bowl, stir together flour, baking powder, and salt.

2. Cut in butter until crumbly. Stir in milk and blend well to make a soft dough. Really, what you are making is biscuit dough.

3. Divide dough in half. Roll each piece into an oval the size of your slow cooker crock.

4. Grease slow cooker. Place one piece of dough in bottom of the inner crock.

5. Spread the apples over the bottom crust. Sprinkle with cinnamon and nutmeg.

6. Place second pastry crust lightly on top of apples.

7. Use a silicone or plastic knife to cut down through all the layers, making one long cut down the middle and at least 6 cuts side to side.

8. Separately, stir together sugar and boiling water. Pour evenly over dough and apples.

9. Cover and cook on Low for 4 hours until apples are tender.

Why I like this recipe —
   This is the first apple recipe I make when the air feels chilly in the fall and I'm ready for lots of spice and baked treats. I serve it warm from the cooker with vanilla ice cream. Enjoy!

Apple Coconut Pudding

Makes 4-6 servings

Prep. Time: 15 minutes ❧ Cooking Time: 2 hours ❧ Standing Time: 30 minutes

Ideal slow-cooker size: 5-quart

18-oz. butter recipe golden cake mix

1 cup shredded coconut

1 stick (½ cup) butter, at room temperature

6 cups peeled, sliced, firm, baking apples, approximately 6 apples

½ cup chopped walnuts

1 cup water

¼ cup lemon juice

1. Combine dry cake mix and coconut in a large bowl. Cut in butter with pastry cutter.

2. Place sliced apples in lightly greased slow cooker. Sprinkle with walnuts.

3. Sprinkle crumb mixture evenly over apples and walnuts.

4. In a small bowl combine water and lemon juice and pour over top apples and crumbs.

5. Cover and cook on High for 2 hours, until set and apples are soft.

6. Allow to sit for 30 minutes in the turned-off cooker before spooning out into dessert dishes. Lovely with ice cream or whipped cream.

TIP

You can replace the cake mix with 2 cups all-purpose flour, 1½ cups sugar, 1 Tbsp. baking powder, ½ cup powdered milk, and 1 tsp. vanilla.

Why I like this recipe —
    I like to start a dessert in the slow cooker just before I start making dinner. Then it's ready just after we eat, smelling delicious the entire time. The combination of apples and coconut is wonderful here.

Apple-Pear Fruit Crisp

Makes 12 servings

Prep. Time: 15 minutes if you don't peel the fruit ❦ Cooking Time: 2–4 hours

Ideal slow-cooker size: 5-quart

nonstick cooking spray

6 cups cored, sliced apples

6 cups cored, sliced pears

1 cup dried cherries *or* cranberries

2 Tbsp. sugar

1 Tbsp. grated orange peel

3 tsp. ground cinnamon, *divided*

1 cup all-purpose flour

1 cup dry oats, quick *or* rolled

¾ cup brown sugar

1 tsp. ground ginger

¼ tsp. ground mace

1½ sticks (¾ cup) butter, softened

1. Spray slow cooker crock with nonstick cooking spray.

2. In a large bowl, combine apples, pears, cherries or cranberries, sugar, orange peel, and 1 tsp. cinnamon. Toss well.

3. In a separate bowl mix together the flour, oats, brown sugar, ginger, mace, and remaining 2 tsp. cinnamon. Stir to combine.

4. Using a pastry cutter, or 2 knives, cut the pieces of butter into the flour mixture. Continue until the butter turns the mixture into chunky little pellets.

5. Sprinkle the mixture over the fruit.

6. Cover. Cook on High 2–3 hours, or on Low 4 hours, or until the fruit is bubbly.

7. One-half hour before the end of the cooking time, take the lid off so the topping can dry.

8. Serve warm with fresh whipped cream, milk, or ice cream.

Why I like this recipe—

I can't resist fruit crisp—with almost any combination of fruit. I make it for breakfast, supper, dessert. The dried cherries and orange peel set this one apart. You'll see I don't peel the apples and pears. They cook soft, so why bother? Plus the peels harbor some fiber that's worth having. But go ahead and peel yours if you prefer.

Apple Cranberry Crisp

QUICK
and
EASY

Makes 8-10 servings
Prep. Time: 20 minutes ✂ Cooking Time: 4½-4¾ hours
Ideal slow-cooker size: 4-quart

3 cups chopped apples, unpeeled

2 cups raw cranberries

⅓ cup white sugar

1½ cups old-fashioned, *or* quick-cooking oats, uncooked

½ cup brown sugar

⅓ cup all-purpose flour

⅓ cup chopped pecans

1 stick (½ cup) butter, melted

whipped cream, *optional*

1. Combine apples, cranberries, and white sugar in your greased slow cooker. Mix thoroughly to blend everything well.

2. Cover. Cook on Low for 4 hours, or until the apples are as soft as you want.

3. While the apples and cranberries are cooking, combine the oats, brown sugar, flour, pecans, and butter in a good-sized bowl. Mix until the topping turns crumbly. Set it aside.

4. When the apples are finished cooking, scatter the topping over the hot fruit.

5. Continue cooking, uncovered, for 30-45 minutes, or until the topping is warm and beginning to brown around the edges. Serve warm with whipped cream if you wish.

Why I like this recipe—
    This recipe can step in at all kinds of times—when I need a quick breakfast, when I'm looking for a dessert, when it's late on a Saturday or Sunday and I'm not ready to launch a full meal. This is one of those almost-all-purposes dishes.

Pear Ginger Crisp

Makes 4-6 servings
Prep. Time: 20 minutes 　　 Cooking Time: 2½ hours
Ideal slow-cooker size: 3-quart

4 large ripe pears, peeled and sliced

2 Tbsp. sugar

1 Tbsp. lemon juice

1 Tbsp. + ½ cup all-purpose flour, *divided*

½ cup brown sugar

⅔ cup dry oats, quick *or* rolled (rolled have more texture)

¼ tsp. cinnamon

pinch ground cloves

¼ tsp. salt

3 Tbsp. cold butter

2 Tbsp. minced candied ginger

1. In a mixing bowl, gently mix the pears, sugar, lemon juice, and 1 Tbsp. flour together.

2. Place pear mixture in lightly greased slow cooker.

3. In same mixing bowl, cut together remaining ½ cup flour, brown sugar, oats, cinnamon, cloves, salt, butter, and candied ginger.

4. Sprinkle oat topping over pears.

5. Cover and cook on High for 2 hours, until pears are soft. Remove lid and cook on High an additional 30 minutes to crisp up the top.

Why I like this recipe —
Pears are so luscious when they're perfectly ripe that I do usually just eat them out of hand. But if I want a pear dessert, I turn to this one. The candied ginger is a pleasing twist.

TIP

Like most crisps, this one is just perfect with some vanilla ice cream on top.

Perfect Peach Cobbler

Makes 6-8 servings
Prep. Time: 15 minutes   Cooking Time: 2-3 hours
Ideal slow-cooker size: 4- or 5-quart

8 fresh peaches, peeled and sliced

½–1 cup sugar, depending on how sweet you like things

½ cup (1 stick) butter, softened

1 egg, beaten

1 tsp. vanilla

¼ tsp. salt

1 cup all-purpose flour

½ tsp. freshly grated nutmeg

1. Place peaches in lightly greased slow cooker.
2. In a mixing bowl, cream together sugar and butter.
3. Add egg, vanilla, and salt. Beat well.
4. Gradually add flour to creamed mixture.
5. Spread batter over peaches.
6. Sprinkle with nutmeg.
7. Cover and cook on High for 2-3 hours, until middle is set and peach juice is bubbling at the edges.

QUICK
and
EASY

Peaches and Cream Dessert

Makes 6 servings

Prep. Time: 10-15 minutes ⚜ Cooking Time: 2-3 hours ⚜ Standing Time: 30 minutes
Ideal slow-cooker size: 4- or 5-quart

¾ cup all-purpose flour

1 egg

½ tsp. baking powder

½ tsp. salt

3-oz. box instant vanilla pudding

½ cup milk

3 Tbsp. butter, softened

1 qt. sliced peaches, drained,
3 Tbsp. juice reserved

8-oz. pkg. cream cheese, softened

3 Tbsp. peach juice

2 Tbsp. sugar

½ tsp. cinnamon

1. Put flour, egg, baking powder, salt, dry
   pudding, milk, and butter in a mixing bowl.
   Beat well with electric mixer.

2. Pour batter into greased slow cooker.

3. Lay peach halves or slices on top.

4. Mix together cream cheese and 3 Tbsp. peach
   juice. Pour over peaches.

5. Mix sugar and cinnamon together. Sprinkle
   over cream cheese mixture.

6. Cover and cook on High for 2-3 hours, or until
   toothpick inserted in center comes out clean.

7. Allow to stand for 30 minutes with the lid off
   before serving.

Rhubarb Crunch

Makes 6-8 servings
Prep. Time: 20-30 minutes ❧ Cooking Time: 4-5 hours
Ideal slow-cooker size: 3-quart

FILLING INGREDIENTS:

1 quart rhubarb, cut in 1"-pieces

¾ cup granulated sugar

4 Tbsp. all-purpose flour

1 tsp. cinnamon, *optional*

¼ tsp. salt

TOPPING INGREDIENTS:

1 cup dry oatmeal, rolled *or* quick oats

¾ cup brown sugar

¼ cup (half stick) butter, melted

1. Combine all batter ingredients in your greased slow cooker.
2. Cover. Cook on Low 3½-4½ hours.
3. While the filling is cooking, combine dry oatmeal, brown sugar, and butter in a bowl. When the rhubarb is as soft as you like it, sprinkle the topping over top.
4. Continue cooking the Crunch—uncovered—another 30 minutes.
5. Serve warm with milk, whipped cream or whipped topping, or ice cream.

Blueberry Crisp

Makes 6-8 servings
Prep. Time: 15-20 minutes   Cooking Time: 2 hours
Ideal slow-cooker size: 4-quart

½ cup brown sugar

¾ cup dry rolled oats

½ cup whole wheat flour,
or all-purpose flour

½ tsp. cinnamon

dash salt

6 Tbsp. butter, at room temperature

4 cups blueberries, fresh *or* frozen

2–4 Tbsp. sugar, depending on
how sweet you like things

2 Tbsp. instant tapioca

2 Tbsp. lemon juice

½ tsp. grated lemon peel

1. In a large bowl, combine brown sugar, oats, flour, cinnamon, and salt. Cut in butter using a pastry cutter or two knives to make crumbs. Set aside.

2. In a separate bowl, stir together blueberries, sugar, tapioca, lemon juice, and lemon peel.

3. Spoon blueberry mixture into greased slow cooker. Sprinkle crumbs over blueberries.

4. Cover and cook on High for 1½ hours. Remove lid and cook an additional 30 minutes on High.

Curried Fruit Mix

Makes 8-10 servings

Prep. Time: 10 minutes ❧ Cooking Time: 3-4 hours ❧ Standing Time: 2-8 hours

Ideal slow-cooker size: 3½- or 4-quart

15-oz. can peaches, undrained

15-oz. can apricots, undrained

15-oz. can pears, undrained

20-oz. can pineapple chunks, undrained

15-oz. can black cherries, undrained

½ cup brown sugar

1 tsp. curry powder

3-4 Tbsp. quick-cooking tapioca, depending upon how thickened you'd like the finished dish to be

1 Tbsp. butter *or* margarine, *optional*

1. Combine fruit in a mixing bowl. Let stand for at least 2 hours, or up to 8, to allow flavors to blend. Drain. Place in slow cooker.

2. Add remaining ingredients. Mix well. Top with butter, if you want.

3. Cover. Cook on Low 3-4 hours.

4. Serve warm or at room temperature.

Slow Cooker Crème Brulee

Makes 4-6 servings

Prep. Time: 20 minutes   ❦   *Cooking Time: 2-4 hours*   ❦   *Chilling Time: 5 hours*
Ideal slow-cooker size: 6-quart oval

5 egg yolks

2 cups heavy cream

½ cup sugar

1 Tbsp. high-quality
vanilla

pinch salt

¼ cup super-fine sugar

fresh berries, to garnish

TIP

This is a perfect summer dessert if you don't have an ice-cream maker but still want to make something cold and creamy.

1. Get a baking dish that fits in your slow cooker. Put it in the slow cooker and pour water around it until the water comes halfway up the sides of the dish. Push the dish down if you need to (as it would be when it's full of the Creme Brulee), to see the water level. Remove the dish and set aside.

2. In medium mixing bowl, beat egg yolks.

3. Slowly pour in cream and sugar while mixing. Add vanilla and salt.

4. Pour mixture into the baking dish.

5. Carefully place dish into water in slow cooker, being careful not to get water in the cream mixture.

6. Cover cooker and cook on High for 2–4 hours, until set but still a little jiggly in the middle.

7. Very carefully remove hot dish from hot slow cooker and let it cool on the counter. Refrigerate for 2 hours.

8. Sprinkle the super-fine sugar evenly over the top. Broil for 3–10 minutes, until the sugar is bubbly and browning. Watch carefully! Or if you own a kitchen torch, use that instead to caramelize the sugar.

9. Return Crème Brulee to refrigerator for at least 2 more hours. Serve cold with a few beautiful berries to garnish.

Why I like this recipe —
    It's so simple and so beautiful. I know there are lots of fun additions
to crème brulee, but I rarely tamper with its elegance.

Slow-Cooked Rice Pudding

Makes 4-6 servings

Prep. Time: 5 minutes ❧ Cooking Time: 5-6 hours ❧ Standing Time: 30 minutes

Ideal slow-cooker size: 3- or 4-quart

1–2 Tbsp. butter

¾ cup uncooked white long-grain rice

½ tsp. ground nutmeg

pinch cinnamon

⅔ cup sugar

¼ tsp. salt

5–6 cups milk

whipped cream

maraschino cherries

1. Rub the butter in the lower half of the slow cooker crock to grease it.

2. Place rice, nutmeg, cinnamon, sugar, salt, and 5 cups milk in slow cooker.

3. Cook on Low for 5–6 hours, stirring every 1-2 hours. Add the additional cup of milk if there's not enough liquid for a creamy consistency.

4. Pour pudding into serving bowl. Allow to cool to room temperature at least 30 minutes, or chill before serving. Serve with whipped cream and maraschino cherries.

Why I like this recipe —
This is an easy, easy dessert and so comforting. Of course, you can serve it with other toppings or just by its own delicious self. One of my friends chops up Halloween candy bars and sprinkles them on top of warm rice pudding, letting the chocolate melt a bit before eating.

Strawberry Rhubarb Sauce

QUICK and EASY

Makes 4 quarts

Prep. Time: 15 minutes ❧ *Cooking Time: 3–4 hours* ❧ *Chilling Time: 3 hours*
Ideal slow-cooker size: 4-quart

6 cups rhubarb, diced

6 cups water

½ cup minute tapioca

6-oz. pkg. strawberry gelatin

1½ cups sugar

1 quart fresh strawberries, chopped

1. Place rhubarb, water, and tapioca in slow cooker.
2. Cover and cook on Low until rhubarb is soft and mixture has thickened, 3–4 hours.
3. Stir in gelatin to dissolve. Add sugar and mix well.
4. Pour into pretty glass bowl. Refrigerate.
5. When partly cooled, in about 30 minutes, fold in strawberries. Chill thoroughly, at least 2½ hours.
6. Serve with waffles, vanilla pudding, or cheesecake. Also good eaten as a breakfast side dish or spooned over baked oatmeal.

Everyday
From-Scratch Basics

Homemade Yogurt, page 368

QUICK
and
EASY

Slow Cooker Basic Beans

Makes 6 cups

Prep. Time: 5 minutes ❦ Cooking Time: 3–6 hours ❦ Standing Time: 1 hour or so
Ideal slow-cooker size: 5-quart

2 cups dried beans
such as navy, black,
kidney, *or* pinto

7 cups water

TIP

If you like your beans
soft, do not add salt or
anything acidic to them
until they are finished
cooking as soft as you like
them. The salt and acid
keep the beans
firm.

1. Rinse the dried beans and pick out any stones or debris.

2. Place beans in slow cooker. Add water.

3. Cover and cook on Low for 3–6 hours. The amount of time and water depends on the age of the bean (older will take longer and more water), how hot your cooker cooks, and how soft you like your beans. Fortunately, you have a long grace period with a slow cooker!

4. Start checking the beans at 3 hours. You might need to add more water to keep it just level with the beans.

5. When beans are cooked to the tenderness you want, remove hot crock from electrical base, remove lid, and allow beans to cool if you have time. They're easier to handle when they've cooled off!

6. Portion beans and their cooking liquid in containers. Keep in the refrigerator for up to a week, or freeze for several months.

Cook's Notes —

- *Sometimes I add a bay leaf or a chopped onion, depending on what I have in mind for the finished beans. But often, I am simply cooking beans to store them in the freezer for future recipes instead of buying canned beans, which are more expensive and high in sodium.*

- *Another way to freeze the beans is to strain off the liquid entirely and spread them in a single layer on a baking sheet. Freeze. When the beans are frozen, scrape them into a freezer bag and return to the freezer. Then you can scoop out the amount you need.*

Chicken or Beef Stock

Makes 20 cups

Prep. Time: 10 minutes ❦ *Cooking Time: 12-36 hours* ❦ *Chilling Time: 1-2 hours*
Ideal slow-cooker size: 6-quart

3 lbs. chicken parts, such as backs, necks, and wings, *or* meaty beef bones

1–2 onions, unpeeled, cut in chunks

3 garlic cloves, unpeeled

1 tsp. salt

5 peppercorns

1 bay leaf

1 Tbsp. vinegar

water

1. Place all ingredients in slow cooker, adding water to come up to 1″ from top of crock.

2. Cover and cook on Low for at least 12 hours and up to 36, adding more water as needed. Especially large beef bones will need the full 36 hours to fully extract the good stuff.

3. Allow stock to cool for an hour or two before straining. The bones will be so tender that they will break as you press on the solids to extract the stock. This is good! Be sure to include any marrow if you are using large beef bones.

4. To de-fat the stock, either use a fat separator to strain off fat, or else refrigerate the stock. When it has chilled, the fat will be in a solid layer on top. Lift off the fat with a shallow spoon and discard it.

5. Store stock in fridge for up to a week, or portion it out and freeze it for several months.

TIP

Some people do not care for the smell of stock cooking; you can set your slow cooker in your garage, basement, or other space removed from the kitchen. Just be sure to write yourself a note to check on it at regular intervals!

Cook's Notes —

- *If you roasted a chicken or turkey, save the carcass and make stock from that. The roasting makes for extra-flavorful stock.*

- *Don't skip the vinegar: its presence is not detected in the flavor, but rather in its ability to help extract the minerals and good stuff from the bones.*

Vegetable Broth

Makes 10 cups

Prep. Time: 15 minutes ❦ *Cooking Time: 8½–10½ hours*

Ideal slow-cooker size: 6-quart

1 yellow onion, unpeeled, cut in chunks

1 large potato, unpeeled, cut in chunks

2 carrots, unpeeled, cut in chunks

1 Tbsp. oil

3 dried mushrooms, such as shiitake

2 ribs celery, diced

2 bay leaves

8 peppercorns

2 Tbsp. soy sauce

9 cups water

1 cup white wine

TIP

If you prefer, you can skip the wine and use another cup of water instead.

TIP

You can skip the roasting step if you wish, but the broth will not be as deeply flavored or colored.

1. Mix onion, potato, and carrots together with oil and spread on baking sheet. Roast at 400° for 20–30 minutes, stirring twice, until softened and browned in spots.

2. Scrape vegetables into slow cooker, being sure to get all the browned bits.

3. Add rest of ingredients.

4. Cover and cook on Low 8–10 hours. Remove crock from electrical unit and remove lid. Allow to sit for up to an hour to cool.

5. Strain the broth through a mesh strainer, pressing on the solids in the strainer to get all the good liquid out. Discard solids.

6. Store in refrigerator for up to 1 week, or portion out and freeze for several months.

Why I like this recipe —
I understand the process for making meat stocks, but I was curious about how vegetables gave up their juices for broth. Turns out, the process is not that hard, and the results are delicious.

Hot Bacon Dressing

QUICK
and
EASY

Makes 3-4 cups

Prep. Time: 15 minutes ⏱ Cooking Time: 2½–3½ hours
Ideal slow-cooker size: 2-quart

½ lb. bacon, chopped	1. Fry bacon in a skillet until crisp. Scrape it and the drippings into the slow cooker.
2 cups water	
¾ cup apple cider vinegar	2. Whisk together remaining ingredients until smooth.
1 cup sugar	3. Stir into bacon pieces and drippings.
1 Tbsp. prepared mustard	4. Cover and cook on High for 2–3 hours, until thickened and bubbly, stirring twice.
2 eggs	
4 Tbsp. flour	5. Serve warm over lettuce, spinach, or early spring dandelion greens.

Poached Chicken

Makes 5-6 cups

Prep. Time: 5 minutes ❦ Cooking Time: 1½-3 hours ❦ Chilling Time: 30 minutes
Ideal slow-cooker size: 4-quart

6 boneless, skinless chicken breasts

★ **14-oz. can low-sodium chicken broth**

★ TO MAKE YOUR OWN BROTH, SEE PAGE 357.

1. Place chicken and broth in slow cooker.
2. Cover and cook on Low for 1½-3 hours, until chicken registers 165° on a meat thermometer. Start checking at 1½ hours and do not overcook.
3. Remove chicken from poaching broth with slotted spoon. Set on cutting board until cool enough to handle, about 30 minutes. Chop. Or store whole breasts in fridge in poaching broth.

TIP
To freeze the chicken for later, chop or shred it into portions. Include a tablespoon or two of the poaching broth and freeze.

Simply (Wonderful) Cooked Chicken

QUICK
and
EASY

Makes 4-4½ cups
Prep. Time: 15-20 minutes ❧ Cooking Time: 3½ to 10 hours
Ideal slow-cooker size: 5-quart

2 carrots, sliced

2 onions, sliced

2 celery ribs, cut in 1"-thick pieces

3-lb. chicken, whole *or* cut up

1 tsp. salt

½ tsp. dried coarse black pepper

1 tsp. dried basil, *optional*

½ cup water, chicken broth, *or* white cooking wine

1. Put the vegetables into the bottom of your slow cooker.

2. Set the chicken on top.

3. Sprinkle with the seasonings.

4. Pour the liquid down along the side of the cooker so you don't wash the seasonings off.

5. Cover. Cook on Low 8-10 hours, or on High 3½-5 hours. (Use 1 cup liquid if you're cooking on High.)

6. When you're done cooking, lift the chicken out onto a platter. Allow it to cool and then debone it. Strain the solids out of the broth and save the broth for your next soup or rice dish.

Why I like this recipe —
    You've got fully cooked chicken, plus broth that is a great foundation for soups—chicken noodle, chicken vegetable... And it's cooked itself while you were off doing other things.

Millet in the Slow Cooker

Makes 4 cups

Prep. Time: 5 minutes ❧ *Cooking Time: 6-9 hours*

Ideal slow-cooker size: 2- or 3-quart

1 cup millet

4 cups water

½ tsp. salt, *optional*

1. Place millet, water, and optional salt in slow cooker.

2. Cover and cook on Low 6–9 hours until millet is fluffy and water is mostly absorbed.

3. Drain off and discard any water remaining. Cooked millet will keep up to two weeks in the fridge, or it can be frozen.

TIP

Use cooked millet in recipes that call for cooked rice, or serve hot with a pat of butter as a side dish.

Cook's Note —

What can you do with cooked millet? Serve hot with milk, honey, and fruit for breakfast. Add to soups instead of rice or barley. Chill and add veggies and dressing to make a sturdy salad.

Wheat Berries (or Farro or Spelt or Rye or Barley) in the Slow Cooker

QUICK and EASY

Makes 4 cups

Prep. Time: 5 minutes ✂ Cooking Time: 4–12 hours
Ideal slow-cooker size: 3- or 4-quart

1 cup wheat berries, farro, spelt, rye, or hulled/pearl barley

3 cups water

¼ tsp. salt, optional

1. Place wheat berries or other grain, water, and optional salt in slow cooker.

2. Cover and cook on Low 8–12 hours or High 4–5 hours. The wheat berries are done when they are soft and chewy. There may be water left that can just be drained off and discarded.

Cook's Note —

Cooked wheat berries will keep in the fridge for up to 2 weeks, or they can be frozen. Make a sturdy salad with wheat berries. They are also nice reheated for breakfast with milk and honey, served instead of rice at dinner, and used as a ground meat extender in recipes like meat loaf or chili.

Easy Ketchup

Makes 3 cups
Prep. Time: 25 minutes ∷ *Cooking Time: 7-10 hours*
Ideal slow-cooker size: 5-quart

2 pounds very ripe red tomatoes
1 large onion, coarsely chopped
2 celery ribs, coarsely chopped
1 red bell pepper, coarsely chopped
¼ cup apple cider vinegar
¼ cup red wine vinegar
1 garlic clove, crushed
1 Tbsp. honey
1 Tbsp. brown sugar
1 tsp. Dijon mustard
⅛ tsp. ground cloves
⅛ tsp. celery seed
⅛ tsp. ground allspice
⅛ tsp. ground cinnamon
½ teaspoon salt
pinch red pepper flakes

1. Combine all ingredients in blender or food processor and process until entirely smooth.
2. Pour into slow cooker.
3. Cover and cook on High for 1 hour to get it hot.
4. Turn cooker to Low and prop lid open at one end with a wooden spoon handle or chopstick.
5. Stir occasionally, being sure that the condensation on the lid does not drip back down into the Ketchup when you move the lid. You are thickening the Ketchup by evaporating the water out of it. Cook on Low for 6-9 hours, until it has thickened and gotten darker.
6. Taste the Ketchup and add more spices, sugar, or salt if you wish.
7. Store Ketchup in fridge for several months. Ketchup can be canned by following guidelines from the USDA or other reputable source.

Why I like this recipe —
I'm recalling my childhood when my mother boiled down vats of ketchup to can. However, that was a big kitchen commitment with lots of splatters and stirring. Making ketchup in the slow cooker is so much easier! I don't need to pay much attention to it, and I can make a small batch and it will keep fine in the fridge.

Pear Honey

QUICK and EASY

Makes 4 cups

Prep. Time: 15 minutes ✿ Cooking Time: 4–6 hours ✿ Chilling Time: 1–2 hours

Ideal slow-cooker size: 3- or 4-quart

10 medium-large very ripe pears

1½ cups unsweetened crushed pineapple in natural juice

½ cup sugar

½ cup brown sugar

1 Tbsp. lemon juice

1. Peel and core pears. Grind in food chopper or food processor. Place purée in slow cooker.
2. Add pineapple, pineapple juice, and sugar. Mix.
3. Cook 4–6 hours on Low, stirring occasionally, and occasionally venting the lid with a wooden spoon handle or chopstick to allow mixture to thicken and cook down.
4. Stir in the lemon juice.
5. Allow to cool to warm with the lid off, 1–2 hours. Divide among jars. Pear Honey will keep in the refrigerator for several weeks, or it may be frozen.

TIP

Use Pear Honey as you would jam or honey: on toast, stirred into hot tea, or drizzled on plain cake.

Why I like this recipe—

When pears get ripe, they are perfectly ripe for such a short period of time, and they are so luscious. I've found this recipe is a good way to indulge my love of pears and not waste any if I bought more than we could eat.

QUICK
and
EASY

Slow-Cooked Apple Butter

Makes 6-8 cups
Prep. Time: 20-30 minutes ❧ Cooking Time: 8-8½ hours
Ideal slow-cooker size: 4-quart

12 apples
¼–⅓ cup water
½ cup sugar
2 tsp. cinnamon
½ cup brown sugar

1. Wash, core, and peel apples. Cut into quarters. Place in slow cooker.

2. Mix all other ingredients together well in a bowl, using the lesser amount of water. Pour over the apples and stir together. You may need to add more water during the cooking process, depending on how juicy your apples are.

3. Cook on Low 8 hours, or until the mixture smells deep and darkly sweet. Check to see if the apple butter is thick enough for you. If you want it to be thicker, cook it with the lid off for 30 minutes or so to evaporate more moisture.

4. Store in fridge for up to 2 weeks, or otherwise freeze it or can it according to your canner's instructions.

Why I like this recipe —
We eat this spread on toast and over cottage cheese. I also love it in toasted cheese sandwiches. Spread it on the inside of the bottom bread slices before topping them with cheese.

Homemade Applesauce

Makes 12-15 servings
Prep. Time: 30 minutes ❦ Cooking Time: 5-9 hours
Ideal slow-cooker size: 6-quart

cooking spray

10–14 large apples, several different kinds preferred

¼ cup water

sugar, *optional*

1. Lightly spray the inside of the slow cooker crock.

2. Peel, core and chop the apples.

3. Place the apples and water in the slow cooker. The apples should come to the top of the crock.

4. Cover and cook on Low for 5-9 hours, stirring once or twice. The time depends on the ripeness and varieties of the apples. When the apples can easily be smashed against the side of the inner crock with the cooking spoon, turn off the heat.

5. Use an immersion blender or a handheld masher to mash or blend the apples until you make an applesauce as smooth as you like— some people prefer a purée, and others like some chunks.

6. Taste the applesauce to see if you want to add any sugar. This also depends on the varieties of apples you used and on personal taste. Add the sugar while the applesauce is hot so it dissolves easily.

7. Pour applesauce into a bowl to cool. Serve warm, at room temperature, or chilled. Applesauce may be frozen for several months. It will keep in the fridge for up to a week.

Homemade Yogurt

Makes 8½ cups

Prep. Time: 15 minutes ❧ *Cooking Time: 2½ hours*
Standing Time: 3 hours, and then 8-12 hours
Ideal slow-cooker size: 3- or 4-quart

½ gallon (8 cups)
2% *or* whole milk

½ cup plain
yogurt with
live cultures,
or freeze-dried
yogurt starter

TIP

Add sweeteners,
flavors, and fruit just
before eating, to the
individual taste of
each person.

1. Place milk in slow cooker. Cover and cook on Low for 2½ hours.

2. Turn the cooker off and unplug it, but keep the lid on. Allow to sit in this manner for 3 hours.

3. The milk should be in the lukewarm range (105–115°) before you introduce the yogurt cultures. If you're unsure, check it with a kitchen candy thermometer.

4. Scoop a cup of the lukewarm milk into a small mixing bowl. Add the yogurt or yogurt starter. Whisk well.

5. Return the milk/yogurt mixture to the slow cooker. Whisk again to distribute the starter through all of the milk.

6. Put the lid on. Swaddle the entire, unplugged slow cooker in a beach towel or two. Allow to sit for 8–12 hours undisturbed.

7. The yogurt should be thick and gelatinous. It will thicken more with chilling or a longer incubation (but it will get more tart the longer it is incubated!). Gently scoop the yogurt into containers, but try to avoid stirring it as that breaks down its natural gel and it will get runnier.

8. Refrigerate. Keeps in the fridge for 2–3 weeks, but it gets more tart as it ages. You can use ½ cup homemade yogurt as the starter for the next batch, although some people think it's helpful to renew the starter with a commercial yogurt every few batches or so.

Cook's Notes —

- Make Greek yogurt with your homemade yogurt: line a mesh strainer with cheesecloth and set it over a bowl. Pour yogurt into the lined strainer. Allow the whey to strain out, into the bowl. Allow to strain for 1 hour or up to 12 hours for really thick yogurt (yogurt cheese, some people call it, and use it like cream cheese). The whey is quite nutritious and can be used instead of buttermilk for some baked goods.

- Another thickening option is to add a packet of unflavored, powdered gelatin at the end of the yogurt incubation. Whisk it gently through the yogurt, and after it's been refrigerated for a few hours, the yogurt will set up more firmly.

Homemade Cream of Mushroom Soup — on the stove

Makes about 1¼ cups (10 oz.)

3 Tbsp. butter

¼ cup mushrooms, chopped

1 Tbsp. onion, chopped

3 Tbsp. flour

1 cup milk (skim, 1%, 2%, or whole)

1. In a small saucepan, melt butter.
2. Sauté mushrooms and onion in butter until tender. Stir frequently.
3. Add flour and stir until smooth. Cook over low heat for a minute or so to cook off the raw flour taste.
4. Continuing over low heat, gradually add milk, stirring the whole time.
5. Stir frequently to keep soup from sticking. When soup begins to bubble, stir continuously until it thickens to a creamy consistency.

Homemade Cream of Mushroom Soup — in the microwave

Makes about 1¼ cups (10 oz.)

3 Tbsp. butter

¼ cup mushrooms, chopped

1 Tbsp. onion, chopped

3 Tbsp. flour

1 cup milk (skim, 1%, 2%, or whole)

1. In a 1- or 2-qt. microwave-safe container, melt 3 Tbsp. butter on high for 30 seconds.
2. Stir chopped mushrooms and onions into melted butter.
3. Microwave on high for 1 minute, or just enough to make the vegetables tender.
4. Stir in flour until well blended.
5. Microwave on high for 1 minute, just enough to overcome the raw flour taste.
6. Gradually stir in milk until as well blended as possible.
7. Microwave on Power 5 for 45 seconds.
8. Stir until well blended.
9. Microwave on Power 5 for another 45 seconds. The mixture should be starting to bubble and thicken.
10. Stir again until well blended.
11. If the mixture isn't fully bubbling and thickened, microwave on high for 20 seconds.
12. Stir. If the mixture still isn't fully bubbling and thickened, microwave on high for 20 more seconds.
13. Repeat Step 12 if needed.

Cook's Note —

If your microwave is fairly new and powerful, you will probably have a creamy soup by the end of Step 8 or 10 below. If you're working with an older, less powerful, microwave, you will likely need to go through Step 12, and maybe Step 13.

Metric Equivalent Measurements

If you're accustomed to using metric measurements, I don't want you to be inconvenienced by the imperial measurements I use in this book.

Use this handy chart, too, to figure out the size of the slow cooker you'll need for each recipe.

Weight (Dry Ingredients)

1 oz		30 g
4 oz	¼ lb	120 g
8 oz	½ lb	240 g
12 oz	¾ lb	360 g
16 oz	1 lb	480 g
32 oz	2 lb	960 g

Slow Cooker Sizes

1-quart	0.96 l
2-quart	1.92 l
3-quart	2.88 l
4-quart	3.84 l
5-quart	4.80 l
6-quart	5.76 l
7-quart	6.72 l
8-quart	7.68 l

Volume (Liquid Ingredients)

½ tsp.		2 ml
1 tsp.		5 ml
1 Tbsp.	½ fl oz	15 ml
2 Tbsp.	1 fl oz	30 ml
¼ cup	2 fl oz	60 ml
⅓ cup	3 fl oz	80 ml
½ cup	4 fl oz	120 ml
⅔ cup	5 fl oz	160 ml
¾ cup	6 fl oz	180 ml
1 cup	8 fl oz	240 ml
1 pt	16 fl oz	480 ml
1 qt	32 fl oz	960 ml

Length

¼ in	6 mm
½ in	13 mm
¾ in	19 mm
1 in	25 mm
6 in	15 cm
12 in	30 cm

Substitute Ingredients for when you're in a pinch —

For one cup buttermilk—use 1 cup plain yogurt; or pour 1⅓ Tbsp. lemon juice or vinegar into a 1-cup measure. Fill the cup with milk. Stir and let stand for 5 minutes. Stir again before using.

For 1 oz. unsweetened baking chocolate—stir together 3 Tbsp. unsweetened cocoa powder and 1 Tbsp. butter, softened.

For 1 Tbsp. cornstarch—use 2 Tbsp. all-purpose flour; or 4 tsp. minute tapioca.

For 1 garlic clove—use ¼ tsp. garlic salt (reduce salt in recipe by ⅛ tsp.); or ⅛ tsp. garlic powder.

For 1 Tbsp. fresh herbs—use 1 tsp. dried herbs.

For ½ lb. fresh mushrooms—use 1 6-oz. can mushrooms, drained.

For 1 Tbsp. prepared mustard—use 1 tsp. dry or ground mustard.

For 1 medium-sized fresh onion— use 2 Tbsp. minced dried onion; or 2 tsp. onion salt (reduce salt in recipe by 1 tsp.); or 1 tsp. onion powder. *Note: These substitutions will work for meat balls and meat loaf, but not for sautéing.*

For 1 cup sour milk—use 1 cup plain yogurt; or pour 1 Tbsp. lemon juice or vinegar into a 1-cup measure. Fill with milk. Stir and then let stand for 5 minutes. Stir again before using.

For 2 Tbsp. tapioca—use 3 Tbsp. all-purpose flour.

For 1 cup canned tomatoes—use 1⅓ cups diced fresh tomatoes, cooked gently for 10 minutes.

For 1 Tbsp. tomato paste—use 1 Tbsp. ketchup.

For 1 Tbsp. vinegar—use 1 Tbsp. lemon juice.

For 1 cup heavy cream—add ⅓ cup melted butter to ¾ cup milk. *Note: This will work for baking and cooking, but not for whipping.*

For 1 cup whipping cream—chill thoroughly ⅔ cup evaporated milk, plus the bowl and beaters, then whip; or use 2 cups bought whipped topping.

For ½ cup wine—pour 2 Tbsp. wine vinegar into a ½-cup measure. Fill with broth (chicken, beef, or vegetable). Stir and then let stand for 5 minutes. Stir again before using.

"Quick and Easy" Recipe Index

Recipe and Ingredient Index

Each week you can watch

Phyllis Good is the *New York Times* bestselling author whose cookbooks have sold more than 11 million copies. She has more than 600,000 Facebook fans. And now she has a weekly cooking show.

Check it out each week and be engaged, encouraged, and enabled!

 www.Fix-ItandForget-It.com
www.YouTube.com/CookingWithPhyllis

Take a cooking class with Phyllis!

In our Classroom/Kitchen, everyone has a front-row seat, just one step away from the instructor. Most of the classes include food; many are full lunches or full dinners. Come hungry!

Visit our website today for a complete list of our cooking classes:

www.GoodCookingStore.com

Phyllis has always dreamed of having a cooking store which could also offer cooking classes. Her dream has come true!

Because of the shape of our cooking studio, class members get to help and learn.

Here Phyllis leads a class with her daughter Rebecca, who is Manager of the Cooking School.

HOME OF FIX-IT and FORGET-IT® Cookbooks

www.GoodCookingStore.com
877/525-7745

About the Author

Phyllis Good is a *New York Times* bestselling author whose books have sold more than 11 million copies.

With this book, she launches "Phase 2" of her nationally acclaimed *Fix-It and Forget-It* slow-cooker cookbooks, several of which have appeared on *The New York Times* bestseller list, as well as the bestseller lists of *USA Today* and *Publishers Weekly*. In this book, Phyllis adds her voice, offering Tips and personal comments in "Why I like this recipe."

Good has authored many other cookbooks, growing out of her commitment to make it possible for everyone to cook, even if they have too little time or too little confidence. For a complete listing of her books, as well as her blog, and excerpts from and reviews of her books, visit www.Fix-ItandForget-It.com or www.GoodBooks.com.

To learn more about Good's cooking show, "Cooking with Phyllis," see page 382.

My commitment is to make it possible for everyone to cook, even if they have too little time or too little confidence.

Phyllis Good is Executive Editor at Good Books. (Good Books has published hundreds of titles by more than 135 authors.) She received her B.A. and M.A. in English from New York University. She and her husband, Merle, live in Lancaster, Pennsylvania. They have two young-adult daughters, a son-in-law, and one very sweet little grandson.